REBALANCE

Anxiety REBALANCE

CARL VERNON

ALL THE ANSWERS YOU NEED TO OVERCOME ANXIETY & DEPRESSION

headline

First published in Great Britain in 2016
by HEADLINE PUBLISHING GROUP

Originally published in Great Britain in 2015
by Carl Vernon

1

Cataloguing in Publication Data is available from the British Library

Trade Paperback ISBN 978 1 4722 4195 5

Editor: Jane Hammett

Typeset in 9.84/11.66 pt Cambria by Jouve (UK)

Printed and bound in Great Britain by Clays Ltd, St Ives plc

Headline's policy is to use papers that are natural, renewable and recyclable products and made from wood grown in well-managed forests and other controlled sources. The logging and manufacturing processes are expected to conform to the environmental regulations of the country of origin.

HEADLINE PUBLISHING GROUP
An Hachette UK Company
Carmelite House
50 Victoria Embankment
London EC4Y 0DZ

www.headline.co.uk
www.hachette.co.uk

Dedicated to Lisa
The first person I opened up to.
Love, always.

To my daughter
The most precious gift anybody could be given.
You make me grateful every day.

Also dedicated to YOU
For your strength and courage to act.

Disclaimer
All the material provided in *Anxiety Rebalance* is for information or educational purposes only. None of the content is intended to be a substitute for professional medical advice, diagnosis or treatment. You must consult your doctor before deciding to take any action in regards to any of your symptoms or medical conditions. Do not withdraw or partake in any programme or exercise without first consulting your doctor. *Anxiety Rebalance* and its associated products are for adult use only, and any information passed on to minors must be the responsibility and decision of a legal guardian.

Contents

Part 2: Techniques to Reduce Anxiety and Increase Energy

Part 3: Realign Your Focus

Part 4: Ten Actions to Achieve BALANCE

A personal message

I know how much courage it takes to stand up to anxiety and depression, which is why I'm happy (and impressed) you're here.

Your bravery is about to be rewarded by discovering the answers you deserve to know, and the few steps you need to take to completely change your life.

Don't allow anxiety and depression to cause doubt – nobody should have to go through their exhausting and debilitating effects. Happiness and freedom exist, and you and your loved ones deserve the opportunity to get the *real* you back.

Thanks for allowing me to be part of your revival.

Your search stops here.

Carl Vernon

'Everything you've ever wanted is on the other side of fear.'

- George Addair

Introduction

Throw away all your beliefs about anxiety and depression, because I'm about to change the way you think about them for good.

I spent fifteen years living with these conditions, and I've been where you are now. For ten of those years I lived in complete denial, not telling a soul – not even the people closest to me – about the internal torture I went through every minute of every day. Nobody had a clue, and I became an expert at covering up my true thoughts and feelings, convinced I was the only person on the planet going through them. I felt completely isolated and alone, coping with life rather than living it, trying to understand why I'd been cursed with such a debilitating and horrible affliction.

I'll tell you more about my personal experience, but to cut a long story short, anxiety and depression nearly ended my life. Social anxiety, panic attacks, OCD (obsessive compulsive disorder) and agoraphobia were all disorders I battled with daily, in a fight I consistently lost. For years, locking the world away felt like my only option. The smaller my world was, the better – this normally consisted of the four walls of my bedroom, with a blanket pulled over my head.

It's hard to try and sum up just how bad it was in a couple of paragraphs, but I'm assuming you're reading this book because you do know what it feels like, or know somebody going through it. You know how soul-destroying it is, and you want to do something about it. By picking up this book you're doing exactly that, and I'm pleased to say this is your turning point.

Everybody has to have a turning point for real change to happen. For me, it took many years of anguish, confusion, disappointment and despair, but I'm not going to look back and regret the fifteen years of suffering. I'd rather see it as a journey – one I had to take to enable me to help you. I don't regret a day of my struggle because it's allowed me to truly understand what you're going through, and be part of your life right now, armed with the knowledge that change is absolutely possible.

The moment that changed everything for me (my turning point) happened at the supermarket, and I explain it in detail later in the book. It was the biggest step in my revival, and the reason *Anxiety Rebalance* was born. It encouraged me to move forward and continue to find answers – not only for me, but for all the others suffering with the domineering, stubborn and paralysing conditions that are anxiety and depression.

Why I wrote this book

I didn't want this book to be like all the others out there. A big reason for that is they didn't offer me the answers I craved. It's important to me you know that, because if your search for a solution is anything like mine was, you've probably been left wondering if a solution exists at all. You'll know as well as I do that mental health disorders are one of the most debilitating and horrible conditions anybody can suffer from. Answers are the one thing sufferers yearn for, and when I was searching I couldn't find them. For all the information the internet offered, all the books the library held, the years of medical schooling my doctor had and training my counsellor possessed, *real* answers were just not there. I'd hear the same tired information repeated over and over again:

'It's just anxiety, Carl; don't worry.'

'I can show you a cure that's guaranteed to eliminate it.'

'Take these pills and give it twelve weeks.'

'Distract yourself by turning your music up and forget about it.'

'Get a grip!'

I tried therapy, medication, read hundreds of self-help books, watched DVDs and listened to endless CDs – I must have completed all the methods available on the market. Wading through all the rubbish was a lengthy and impossible task. The more advice I was given, the more disillusioned I felt. Help and information seemed to be stuck in the Stone Age! What was clear was the number of companies willing to take advantage of my vulnerability. A particular pet hate of mine was the 'money back' guarantee.

WE WILL CURE YOU – OR YOU GET YOUR MONEY BACK!

You expect a 'money back' guarantee on a dishwasher, but not on your state of mind! For me, this summed up what a mess I was in. All of us sufferers desperately seeking a cure didn't stand a chance. Websites I read seemed to battle over which could take the most money from vulnerable people using hard sales techniques. Celebrity endorsements and testimonials were there to entice and convince you, along with promises of a 'cure' and 'elimination', which were completely untrue and misleading. My doctor could only ever offer me two options: medication and CBT (cognitive behavioural therapy), neither of which offered a long-term solution and freedom. Nobody *truly* understood what I was going through. Patience and time were quickly running out.

Was there a cure?

Are short-term fixes the best I could hope for?

Would I have to live with this condition for the rest of my life?

These were just a few of the questions that buzzed around in my head all day, every day. My optimism had faded years ago, and I had nothing left in the tank. I felt let down. I was in such a fragile state of mind I had no idea who or what to trust.

There were periods of time when I thought I'd found a 'cure' and made significant progress, only for anxiety and depression to come back even more strongly, which was devastating, to say the least. Ultimately, nothing worked, and I was constantly let down and disappointed. I ran out of options and didn't know where to turn for help – I just wanted answers.

If I could relate to so many other people's experiences, and knowing how common mental health conditions are, why wasn't there anything out there that helped?

I knew first-hand how stubborn anxiety and depression can be, but I couldn't understand why a *real* solution didn't exist.

Time for change

My favourite quote is by Albert Einstein:

'Insanity: Doing the same thing over and over again and expecting different results.'

In my opinion, this summed up how we have dealt with mental health for so long. A revolution was needed to create change.

I'm naturally quite stubborn and very tenacious – I'd have to be to put up with anxiety and depression for fifteen years! A friend once said to me that I like to play devil's advocate, and I'd agree. I like to challenge the status quo, and if I don't believe in something I'm likely to say so, even if everybody else doesn't agree with me. I'm glad I was blessed with this quality (or flaw, as my partner would describe it) because I needed to use every ounce of it to find answers and challenge current methods.

Without going into a philosophical debate, there are lots of things in life we just accept to be the norm because we're told that's just the way things are. For me, dealing with anxiety and depression topped this list.

If you're willing to stick by old methods and practices that never worked in the first place, how are you ever going to change them? Change was exactly what I needed, and through sheer frustration at the lack of quality information, honest answers and genuine help available, I made it my goal to find the answers myself.

I'm now delighted to be able to offer these answers to you.

About me

We're about to embark on a journey together, so it's only right you get to know me a little better. Throughout the book I discuss lots of my personal experiences, and I'm sure you'll be able to relate to most of them. Being able to relate to other people's experience and discovering that I wasn't alone was a massive relief for me, so I hope you find the same comfort. I don't mind admitting that I'm naturally a private person, but I recognise how important it is to share and put things out in the open, so I thought I'd begin by giving you my life history, including the experiences that have brought me here today. Let's start with one of my earliest memories.

1986

I'm five. Mum is tired of my father's physical abuse, and doesn't feel she has any other choice but to leave my dad after over fifteen years of marriage. She packs a few bags, and takes me and my three brothers with her. Most of her family is based in Leicester, so we naturally head in that direction, although, on arrival, support is distinctly lacking, as we end up homeless. My two eldest brothers decide to lessen my mum's burden and return to my dad in Peterborough, leaving my mum with my little brother (aged three) and me. We ended up staying in a hostel called Border House, all of us having to share one bed. I remember how itchy the blanket was, and how noisy the cars were as they passed the window. It wasn't a nice place, with other families in the same desperate situation as we were in. Even at such a young age I felt anxious, but didn't know how to describe my feelings at the time.

1988
Years of hardship and struggle took their toll, and my mum had a breakdown. Aged seven, I remember the specific moment it happened. We'd just bought a new TV, and the stand needed to be screwed into it. Mum was struggling to get the screw in the hole. As she continued to fiddle with the screw, it fell into a hole, out of reach. She collapsed, her hands over her face, crying uncontrollably, sobbing about how useless she was. The crying continued for what seemed like hours. The rest is a bit of a blank, but I remember being taken into care that night. Mum was hospitalised, and my little brother and I went to stay with foster parents. It was a horrible experience. I didn't think that they were nice people, which was sad because you expect more from people who take in vulnerable kids. We were there for months, and they never made us feel welcome. I felt like an outsider, isolated and alone, never part of their family. Their two children certainly made sure of that. Whenever they sat down to watch a movie, they didn't want me or my brother to sit in the same room. Their parents would have to force them to allow us to sit with them, which of course made my brother and me feel even worse, especially when they scowled at us. Overall, it was a very unpleasant experience that I'm sure laid the foundation for my anxiety later in life.

1993
As a single parent, and someone who had gone through years of physical abuse and mental health issues, Mum worked hard to make sure my brother and I were taken care of, including being well clothed and fed, with a few other luxuries like mountain bikes and computers (even though she couldn't really afford them). She adopted this mentality when trying to get us into one of the best schools in Leicester. It was two bus rides from where we lived, but her boyfriend at the time lived within a mile of the school, so she used his address to get us in.

Aged twelve, my first day at the school was a nightmare. I walked into the classroom and felt all eyes staring at me as the teacher introduced me and another kid as new starters. The other kids started to giggle and I remember feeling extremely paranoid. I wasn't sure what they were laughing at – maybe it was my terrible haircut. The style was called curtains, but I didn't use hair gel, so it just looked like I had a bowl on my head (don't ask for a picture!). I struggled to settle in at first, but I was lucky that the kid starting on the same day as me was in the same boat, so we naturally made friends. He ended up being my best friend, and because he had a lot of street cred, some naturally rubbed off on me, making my schooldays a little more bearable. And I also started to use hair gel.

1995

I was on my way to play football with two of my friends (as a fourteen-year-old boy, this was a usual pastime) when I got a call from my mum. 'Carl, I have to tell you something. It's about your dad. Come home as soon as you can.' There was no way I was missing out on a game of football, so I got her to tell me what it was about on the phone. She told me, 'Your dad died yesterday.' I hadn't seen him for years, so I didn't know how to react to the news. We had never been close – and this had a lot to do with the fact he was an alcoholic. I ended the call and turned to my friends. 'My dad died yesterday,' I told them. They asked me if I was OK, and I said I was. It was the truth. I was shocked, but OK. We kept walking and I continued as normal. Looking back, I suppose it was an abnormal reaction to the news, but just getting on with it was how I dealt with it. This attitude of bottling things up and just getting on with things continued into my adulthood. It was a big part of my survival instinct, but also one of the main reasons why I suffered in silence for as long as I did.

1997

I never got on with school. I hated it. Towards the end of the last year (the most crucial time with exams) I was hardly there. I would always skive and choose to go to my friend's house instead. Don't ask me how, but I managed to get C and D grades in my GCSEs. Pretty good, considering I never paid much attention in class. Unsurprisingly, I left school at sixteen (as soon as I could) without any real plan. I was working part-time at Burger King and enjoyed the money I earned. I always had more money than my friends, who were still in education. I used to think what fools they were for staying at school. Why stay at school when you could earn all this money? I thought. I'm still ambivalent on this point but, being older and wiser, I can now see the obvious benefits of a good education.

I'd always had a strong work ethic. Between the ages of thirteen and fifteen, rather than spend the summer holidays playing with my friends, I worked full-time in a sweet factory as a packer (strictly cash in hand). I used the money to buy designer clothes from my mum's catalogue, and computer games for my PlayStation. I just about had enough spare cash to buy booze and fags from the local convenience store for me and my friends. (One of our friends looked a lot older than he was, so we sent him in to buy them.)

I tried college for a few months, but that didn't work out – I hated it as much as school. I started working at Burger King full-time, but the smell of fat and burgers got to me after a while, so I decided to go and get a 'proper' job. I landed a job as a sales administrator for a sock company. I was still sixteen, but mature for my age. I was tasked with inputting data and making sure that processing the sales was done correctly: nothing too tasking, but it got me using computers and speaking to customers. I had been at the company for about three months when it went into administration. It seemed to happen overnight. I sat at my desk and the bailiffs came in and literally took it from under my nose as I was sitting inputting orders. It wasn't the best of experiences from my first 'proper' job, but it set me up for life in the corporate world.

1998

Coming up to my seventeenth birthday, I got a similar role in sales administration for a company that sold cleaning products. There's nothing else notable to add about it, apart from the fact I experienced my first panic attack at this company. I'd experienced small doses of panic previously, but never a full-blown panic attack. It hit me like a ton of bricks. I was happily going about my day, inputting invoices into the system, when for no apparent reason I started to feel disorientated. As I looked at the computer screen, my head started to spin, I began to shake, I became breathless, I felt nauseous, my mouth went dry, I got a hot flush and sweat began to drip from my forehead.

'What the hell is happening to me?' I wondered. I thought I was dying. My colleagues sitting next to me could see I was in distress and called for the first-aider. He came rushing through the office with a green first-aid box in his hand.

'My name is John; I'm the first-aider. Are you OK?' I wasn't sure how to respond. 'I was just sitting at my computer when I started to feel dizzy and strange.'

One of my colleagues passed me a glass of water, and as I took a sip John told me to put my legs up on the desk (I wasn't sure why, but I think it had something to do with the flow of blood). As my symptoms started to subside, I noticed that five or six people were standing around me, including management. Although I wasn't sure what had happened, I began to feel very embarrassed. I put my legs down and reassured everybody that I was OK. That was far from reality. I was petrified. What had just happened to me? Was there something seriously wrong with me? I was allowed to go home early, and these thoughts, along with many others, buzzed around in my head all evening. I was too embarrassed to mention the incident to anybody and kept it quiet (like I always did). The feeling of embarrassment came back the next day at work, when my colleagues asked if I was OK. Again, I assured them everything was fine, and continued inputting the invoices that I'd missed the day before. About twenty minutes later, the same feeling of disorientation and dizziness came back. I couldn't focus on my computer, but this time, rather than ask for help, I got up and stumbled into the kitchen, panic-ridden. The sweat continued to pour down my face as I stood there, wondering what the hell was going on. Luckily, I had an understanding manager (looking back, I think he suffered from anxiety too), and although I couldn't explain what was going on and why I needed to go home, he let me go with no argument. I got home convinced there was something seriously wrong with me. I was too scared to call the doctor, and thought avoidance was the best solution. *If I don't go to the doctor, there's nothing wrong with me, right?* I called in sick the next day: I was too frightened to go back to work. What if it happened again? What if my colleagues were talking about me? The pressure of being away from work was too much to handle, so I was relieved when the company let me go a few weeks later.

Still only seventeen, my ambition and drive had turned into distress and fear. As time passed, I hardly left my home. My friends would call, asking if I was coming out to meet them. I always had an excuse, and declined their offers. The time between this and me getting my next job is a bit of a blur. I knew I couldn't stay at home – I was running out of excuses and I didn't want the truth to come out. What would people think if they knew about my anxiety and the daily panic attacks I endured? I didn't understand what I was going through, so how would they understand? Desperate, I started applying to jobs advertised in the newspaper. I told myself that my problem must be related to using a computer, so I applied for roles that didn't require the use of one. I got an interview with a guy who ran his own landscaping business. He was looking for a helper. God knows how I did it, but I plucked up the courage to take the two buses needed to get to his house (public transport became a real issue for me). It certainly wasn't one of my best interviews, but I think he was pleased I at least looked normal and relatively sensible, so I got the job. It was minimum wage, with no career prospects, but it got me back into work (without a computer). I took it and agreed to start the following week.

I was experiencing a raft of anxiety-related symptoms at this point in my life, but one of the most prevalent was feeling like the floor was unbalanced, and as if it was swallowing me up. It made me feel dizzy and disorientated, so I used to keep an earplug in one ear, even when I didn't need it. (We used earplugs when we used a chainsaw.) The guy I worked for noticed I kept it in my ear, but didn't say anything. He probably thought I was a bit strange or something. That was fine with me – as long as it helped stop the sensation of the floor swallowing me, I didn't care. As well as the earplug, the only other thing that got me through was how busy and physically demanding the job was. Although I was anxious, I didn't have the time to express it. I was too busy chopping down trees and mowing lawns. I used to come home from work a shade of green: my mum and brother still joke about it. They'd say, 'Here comes the swamp monster.'

2000

Although my anxiety and depression were growing and becoming deeper-rooted day by day, I wasn't allowing them to dictate my life as much as previously, so my confidence was growing as well. After the landscaping job and a few other dead-end roles, I thought it was time to start looking for a career. A job in sales was as good as anything else, I thought, so I started to apply for various sales jobs. Aged eighteen, I got a sales executive job at Nissan, even though I had no sales experience. Two managers interviewed me: one was keen, and the other wasn't. (I could tell that by the fact he looked me straight in the eye and told me he wasn't keen on me in the interview.) The other manager won him over and convinced him to take a chance on me. Good choice – I ended up being the top salesperson in the entire group. I was, by some distance, the youngest salesperson in the company, yet continued to consistently outsell the other experienced salesmen month-on-month. I take particular pride in this, as I was suffering from crippling anxiety and panic attacks at the time.

Part of my job was to park the cars in very tight spaces on the forecourt, normally under the manager's supervision (the same guy who had said he wasn't keen on me). He'd scrutinise every manoeuvre I made, ready to pounce on me whenever I made the slightest mistake. I'd only been driving for about six months at the time, so I'd frequently over-rev the engine. He'd screw up his eyes as he stared at me. I could hear what he was thinking: 'Idiot. If this kid didn't sell the cars he does, I'd get rid of him.' It was a tough and pressurised job, and even though it caused me great anxiety and panic, I enjoyed it. Although I didn't think it at the time, I actually believe anxiety was a big reason for my success. How, I'm not entirely sure, but it was certainly there, part of my life and all my decisions.

I continued this success in sales in my next job, in which I became the number-one sales executive for Marks & Spencer Financial Services in the country, out of around 300 people, all while suffering from severe anxiety. My first day on the job wasn't very successful, though. I had to leave early with stomach cramps. My manager wasn't impressed, and she probably thought I wasn't coming back. She was nearly right. I projectile-vomited in the car park as I walked towards my car – anxiety-related, of course. Anxiety had stopped me from living my life to the full and progressing so far, but I wasn't going to let it ruin this job. I returned the next day and, based on my figures for the next year, I was the best employee in their history. Again, this is an achievement I'm proud of, especially when I consider what I went through on a daily basis, including all the times I had to run to the bathroom when I started to panic, and the disorientated feeling that came over me every time I sat down with a customer. Somehow, I battled through it all.

2002–2008

Marks & Spencer wasn't paying me what I knew I could earn in another industry so, after a year or so, I got my first job in recruitment. A tough industry, highly competitive – not good for anxiety and panic attacks. However, I held my own, and made a successful career out of it. A couple of years went by, and at the age of twenty-two, I decided I wanted my own business. I set it up from scratch, and three highly successful years followed, where I doubled my company turnover year on year. By the third year, I was employing eight people. Little did I know that the worst recession in recent times was about to hit, and hit hard. The recruitment industry fell apart – and so did I. My anxiety went through the roof, and my daily panic attacks quadrupled. Everything came toppling down like a house of cards. I had to make all my staff redundant, which upset me deeply. However, it was either risk another month in business, or become homeless. I'd been homeless and knew how that felt. I had no doubt it would have finished me off.

I'd done everything I could to avoid going to the doctor. I really didn't want to take medication, but at this stage I didn't feel that I had any other option. I'll tell you more about my experience with medication a little later but, to cut a long story short, it was a disaster. Mentally, I was in a place I find hard to describe. I'd been suffering from anxiety and depression for over ten years at this point, and I hadn't told a soul, not even my partner, Lisa. She didn't have a clue what I was going through, which was understandable, because she was also coping with her mum being terminally ill with cancer. We spent long periods of time away from each other while she looked after her mum. Because of the lengthy periods of separation, she didn't know how many hours I spent in bed with the blankets pulled over my head, or how I contemplated suicide because I didn't know where to turn, or that I didn't leave the house because of agoraphobia. I was a master faker, incredibly good at making up stories and hiding the truth. Pretending that everything was OK was the only thing that got me through the day. However, as time went by, the days were getting longer, and my anxiety and depression were getting more extreme. I was convinced I was living in hell.

2009
Lisa and I continued to work in the recruitment industry for a little longer, but things were tough and getting worse. Lisa's mum died after a lengthy battle. Lisa was strong throughout her mum's illness, and I admired her strength and the way she coped with everything. I wish I had the strength to tell her then about my anxiety and depression, but after ten years of hiding the truth, it became my way of living and coping. Plus, with everything else she had to contend with, I thought she didn't need the extra burden.

The recession seemed to drag on, and even though work slowed down, it was still demanding. Mentally, I didn't feel like I could cope, but I still wasn't strong enough to say why. When I didn't want to come in to the office, Lisa just thought I was going through a rough patch because of the recession, and I played along with this. We were barely making enough to pay the bills and were close to losing our home. Somehow, I had to drag myself out of the depths of despair and do something about it, otherwise things would get worse.

Business was almost non-existent, but the bills still came rolling in. The pressure was mounting, so I started to apply for jobs. I didn't have any qualifications, and I'd been self-employed for the past four years, so my options were limited. I got a job with an advertising company as a sales executive. The role required me to spend two weeks training in a hotel near Slough (about two hours from where I lived). The company arranged for a hire car to be dropped off at my home on Sunday evening so I could travel to the hotel ready for a Monday morning start. The car key was posted through my letterbox, and as soon as I saw it I started to panic. I hadn't left my house on my own for some time, and I wasn't sure how I was going to cope. Lisa looked at me in excitement.

'Are you ready for your first day?'

I responded with a fake smile: 'Of course; I can't wait.'

I reluctantly packed my clothes ready for a week's stay, put them in the boot of the hire car, and set off. My heart was pounding. I wasn't ready for this. Nevertheless, I kept driving, smiling and waving at Lisa as I passed her.

A couple of hours later, following a panicky drive, I arrived at the hotel. I stood in the queue at reception, feeling completely on edge; the pain in my chest reminded me why I shouldn't be there.

'Please leave your car key with me at reception and the hire company will pick it up in the morning,' the receptionist told me.

What? was my immediate thought. *I'm stuck in this hotel with no transport, hours away from home! Nobody told me I wouldn't have a car!* I immediately felt trapped. My only option of escape was being taken away from me. I started to panic but kept it together – I could see there were others dropping their car keys off at reception, and I didn't want to make a scene. Trying to stop my hands from shaking, I gave the hotel receptionist the car key and headed for my room.

I didn't sleep a wink that night, and I'm not entirely sure how I got through the next day of training, but I did. The coach brought us back to the hotel about 5.30pm, and we all agreed to meet at 7pm for dinner. I planned to drink a glass of wine before I met them to try and ease my nerves. It didn't work; the alcohol just made me more nervous. I changed my clothes and reluctantly headed downstairs to the restaurant where we agreed to meet. We sat around a large table, about eight of us, making small talk. I was doing my best to join in, but the social anxiety was taking hold. Their voices started to muffle and go quieter. I thought I might have water in my ears, so I pressed them and shook my head a little. It didn't help. Their voices were still muffled, and then my vision began to blur. Somebody asked me a question and I couldn't make out what they'd said. They repeated it. I responded nervously, trying to make a joke out of the fact I'd gone deaf. Inside, things were far from funny: I was in a state of absolute panic. My head felt as though it was filled with cotton wool. I made my excuses and left the table. As I walked back to my room I felt like I was floating on air, almost as though I wasn't in my own body – a very strange and unpleasant sensation. I reached my room and the symptoms still hadn't subsided. I opened my door and things didn't seem real. Everything was cloudy and blurred. Although I'd never taken drugs, my first reaction was that my drink had been spiked, which caused me to panic even more. I later discovered it had nothing to do with drugs, alcohol or any other external cause. This was my first experience of depersonalisation. (For anybody who has experienced depersonalisation, you'll know it's one of the scariest symptoms caused by anxiety. For anybody who hasn't, your body uses this function to protect you when it thinks you're in danger. The best way to describe it is as being in a dream-like state, detached from your body – like an out-of-body experience.)

I sat on my bed, my hands cupping my eyes. I was disorientated and didn't know what to do. As I stood up to go to the bathroom I fell to the ground. I'm not sure how long I was on the floor, but I managed to get up and reach the hotel phone. I dialled reception and told them, 'I've just passed out.' The receptionist asked me to repeat what I'd said.

'I've just passed out and I'm not sure what to do.'

The receptionist told me to sit tight and she would send somebody up to my room. There was a knock at the door a couple of minutes later. It was the hotel manager.

'Are you OK?' he asked.

'I passed out, I'm not sure how long for,' I replied.

He'd already called a paramedic, who showed up a couple of minutes later. As he entered the room, the manager left. The paramedic asked me what had happened, and I told him I'd gone for dinner and had to come back to my room because I didn't feel right, and that I'd passed out but wasn't sure for how long.

'When did you last eat?' was his next question.

I told him I'd eaten at lunchtime. He asked a few other questions, and didn't seem as concerned as I was – I was expecting to be carted off in the ambulance. In fact, I was hoping that would happen, because I wouldn't be alone.

'What's wrong with me?' I asked.

'I'm not sure, but it's probably because you haven't eaten for a while. Guys your age faint all the time. It's quite common.'

Part of me was relieved and glad that he didn't mention or ask anything about anxiety; I didn't want to have to admit that I'd suffered for many years. Plus, I was convinced it was something else, and pinning it to anxiety didn't get me out of the situation. He did a few other tests, including checking my blood pressure, and was happy that I didn't need any further attention. By this point, my symptoms had started to subside, but I didn't want to be left on my own. Before I could express my concerns, he was leaving.

As he left and the door shut behind him, I started to cry. I'm not one to cry – it's very rare for me. Something was very wrong. I picked up my phone. I wanted to call Lisa, badly, but I put the phone back down on the bed. I was way too upset to talk to her. She would hear it in my voice, and I couldn't take that chance. Then it started to dawn on me that I was stuck in this hotel room, with no car, and no way to escape. An extreme feeling of panic consumed me, like nothing I'd experienced before. I knew there was no way I could stay there on my own that night. I was scared that I would pass out again. Crazy thoughts like *I don't want to die in this hotel room* ran through my head. I picked up my phone again, and dialled Lisa's number. She picked up.

'Hi, how's it going?'

I paused, trying to hold back the tears and fight the lump in my throat.

'Hello?' she said again, wondering if I was still on the line.

'Hi. It's not great,' I said, trying to speak normally.

'Why, what's wrong?' she replied.

I couldn't think of anything to say, so there was a slight pause again. It was getting too close to her finding out about me crying and being upset, so I made out as though I wasn't feeling well, which would explain the croaky voice. 'I'm not feeling well, and the training isn't great.'

She responded enthusiastically to try and keep me upbeat: 'Don't worry; it's only your first day. See how you feel tomorrow. I bet you'll enjoy it.' Over ten years of hiding the truth wasn't going to be overcome now, so I reluctantly agreed that I'd stay and give it another go. We ended the call agreeing we would talk the next day. I put the phone down and instantly began to sob. Lisa was the only person who could come and rescue me: I was completely alone. I continued to cry for about five minutes until I couldn't take any more. I did something completely out of character. I picked up my phone and called Mum. I'd never gone to anybody for help, including Mum. I had always been way too proud, and had managed to sweep things under the rug wherever possible, and bottle things inside. This time it was different.

'Hello?' she answered. Before I knew it, I was sobbing uncontrollably, unable to get my words out properly.

'I'm stuck in a hotel… I don't know what to do… Lisa doesn't understand…' My mum was shocked to receive a call like this from me, and although she tried to stay calm, I could tell she was extremely worried.

'Sit tight. I'll call Lisa and call you back, OK?'

I agreed and, a few minutes later, Lisa called me. At first, I didn't want to answer the phone. Although I was upset and in distress, I also felt embarrassed – what was I going to say? I answered, still sobbing.

'Carl, what's wrong?' she asked.

I explained that I'd passed out and didn't feel right, but she knew there was something else going on. She agreed to come and pick me up. While I waited, I sat on the bed trying to figure out what I was going to say when she arrived. My anxiety was a dirty little secret I didn't want exposed. A knock came at the door, and the thoughts I'd planned in my head went out the window as soon as I opened the door, tears in my eyes. At first, Lisa wasn't sure how to greet me. I can't blame her – she knew me as a tough character who never cried. The person who opened the door was a red-eyed emotional mess. Neither of us said anything as she helped me get my things together. I wasn't sure what to say, and I don't think she wanted to put me in an awkward situation by asking me questions, so we stayed silent. The silence continued as we walked downstairs, arm in arm. I didn't want anybody from the dinner I'd abandoned to see me, but I felt too weak to walk quickly. We got to the car, and I knew this was the 'now or never' moment.

About fifteen minutes into the journey, I decided my ten years of silence had to end.

'I've got something to tell you. I've not been honest with you. I don't fully understand it myself, but I suffer from anxiety.'

I wasn't expecting the understanding response Lisa gave me – not because she was cold-hearted, but because I'd made such a big thing out of it by keeping it bottled inside for so long.

'OK. Don't worry, I'm sure it's nothing we can't deal with.'

These were reassuring words to me when I was feeling so low. I went on to tell her a little more about how it affected my life, and how long I'd suffered. Nothing seemed to surprise her which, again, was a great relief to me. I wasn't entirely sure how she would take it, or how I would take it – saying what was on my mind was a first for me. We got home and I had mixed feelings as my head hit the pillow. On one hand, I was relieved that the truth had come out but, on the other, I was scared about its implications and how it might change our lives. I was too exhausted from the evening's events to continue worrying, and fell asleep.

The next day was a little strange, as I felt both liberated and ashamed at the same time. Putting my anxiety and depression out in the open made me feel vulnerable at first, but it also made me appreciate that I needed help. I sat at my computer and started to research anxiety for the first time. Reading other people's experience and stories was an unbelievable experience. For years, I had been convinced I was the only person on the planet who suffered from anxiety, yet all these other people had experienced the exact same things I had. Tears came to my eyes, and a lump developed in my throat. I couldn't believe it – I wasn't alone.

2011 onwards
As the years went by, the decision to open up and tell the truth about my anxiety and depression turned out to be one of the best I'd ever made. It's one of the reasons you're reading this now, and along with my experience in the supermarket (you'll read about this shortly), it was fundamental to my revival.

It's now 2015, and I'm about to finish this book after working on it for four years. I hope to use it, along with talks and workshops, to help you and other sufferers of anxiety and depression achieve the same level of revival I have.

Today, I live a life I never thought possible. I have good and bad days, like everybody else, but I'm safe in the knowledge that anxiety and depression will never make me suffer like they did in the past. I proved this earlier this year when I decided to go to Las Vegas (on my own). To some people, of course this isn't a big deal, but to me, having gone through what I did (particularly the hotel incident), it was the ultimate proof that my life had completely changed. For many years, I wouldn't have dreamed such a thing was possible, but I had the time of my life! Being a fan of poker, live shows and last-minute marriages dressed as Elvis, it was the ideal place to confirm my new independent status. I also managed to fulfil an ambition to go back to see the Blue Man Group. Again, the idea of going to a show on my own, especially in Vegas, had once been impossible.

You see, things can change, and by giving you the same knowledge and tools that allowed me to overcome anxiety and depression, my mission is to help you achieve the same life changes I did. Even after everything I went through, including the years of torment and agony, severe panic attacks and social anxiety, OCD and agoraphobia, and being at rock bottom, feeling depressed and suicidal, I can tell you that change is absolutely possible.

The start of your revival

You're going to find I'm a bit of a stickler when it comes to specific words (it's the OCD in me). Lots of people use the word 'recovery' when they refer to overcoming anxiety and depression, but I prefer *revival* – almost as though you're rising from the ashes! 'Repossession' is also good, because you're simply claiming back something you already own.

If you're impatient (like me), you'll want immediate answers. We're going to get to all the answers you need to know, so don't worry about that. In the meantime, there are a couple of bits of information you might like to know:

1. The life you want to live already exists.

2. You already possess all the answers you need.

I expect a few immediate reactions to these statements to be 'Oh no, not more self-help rubbish' or 'If I already possess the answers, why am I reading this book?' But bear with me.

First, let me reassure you that you won't get the usual self-help stuff from me. It didn't work for me, so I wouldn't expect it to work for you. Second, you *really* do already possess the answers you need – all I have to do is help you rediscover them.

There's no doubting the ability of anxiety and depression to permeate your mind, but there *was* a day or a moment in your life when they didn't own you. It might have been recently, when you were playing with your children, watching your favourite TV programme, or when you were sitting on a beach sipping a cocktail. Whenever it was, it proved you already know what it's like to live the life you want – a life built on freedom and choice. It already exists, and it's there waiting for you.

Concentrate on the fact it's already there, rather than on what it takes to get there.

Being highly anxious and feeling depressed will naturally make you doubt yourself and make you believe that revival isn't possible. I know this first-hand. It gets its grubby little paws on you and it's hard to shake it off. That's why, from the very outset, I want you to remember that the life you want to live already exists. You might have to think hard and go back a number of years but, nevertheless, it exists. Anxiety and depression won't like the fact that you possess this knowledge. They'll do their best to keep you locked away in their 'comfort zone' of familiarity, in the belief that you're safe. Sure, staying at home and locking the door is safer than venturing out into the outside world, but what sort of life is that? Being forced to look at the same four walls of your house every day is no way to live – you and I both know that life has so much more to offer.

'Life begins at the end of your comfort zone.'
- Neale Donald Walsch

As I mentioned earlier, in the book you're going to find lots of my personal experiences. Before going through all my sordid secrets (I wish my life had been that interesting!), I'm going to give you an insight into the method behind *Anxiety Rebalance* by highlighting its principles, explaining how it is different from other solutions, and telling you about its ethos. If you like what you read, you can move on to the four parts of this book that will help you get your BALANCE back.

ANXIETY REBALANCE

The principles

These are the principles I stuck to when crafting *Anxiety Rebalance*. They're what make it work, so maybe they could also work for you?

Honesty

When I was searching for answers I was once promised that I would 'never have to face my fears'. I'm sure you agree, this sounds nice, but it's complete rubbish. Anxiety and depression are driven by fear, and one of the first steps you need to take is to face up to them, otherwise they will rule your life for however long you let them. If you're afraid of spiders, how are you ever going to know if you've overcome your fear of them if you continue to avoid them?

One of the big reasons I searched for answers for as long as I did (and didn't find them) was dishonesty. Being impatient and desperate, I wanted the quick fix and miracle cure (like everybody else). That's why I tried so many things. I wanted instant results, but they never came. Nobody was honest enough to tell me it didn't work like that.

Information you want to hear isn't always the information that will help, and dishonesty is the primary reason why other methods fail. My intention is to be 100% honest in this book, which means showing you the good *and* the challenging. It can sometimes be a little hard to take, but that's just because I don't want to mislead you. I want you to benefit from change, and that means me being absolutely honest, including providing facts based on proven evidence and experience.

Simplicity

To quote Albert Einstein again:

***'If you can't explain it simply,
you don't understand it well enough.'***

I completely agree with you, sir! If you have to go to great lengths to talk or write about something, it means you don't really understand it, so I like to keep things simple and concentrate on what you *really* need to know. Besides, if something is perceived as being overcomplicated, there's a high probability you won't do it! As with a crash diet, you might start with good intentions, but they will quickly fade. The more straightforward and simple I keep it, the more likely it is you'll implement all the great tools I'm about to give you.

The perceived complexity that surrounds anxiety and depression is part of the reason we've struggled so long to overcome them. The truth is, it's actually very straightforward: you just need to be shown how to do it using simple language, in the shortest and most effective way possible. You don't need to be bombarded with useless information, technicalities and ten different methods to achieve the same thing. Having a short attention span myself, simplicity is my style. If you're looking for long-drawn-out scientific explanations, you've come to the wrong place! What you will get, however, is answers: answers to questions that would have speeded up my revival and put a stop to the iron grip anxiety and depression had on my life for so many years.

Realism

Over the years I've come across lots of advice: some good, some bad, and some downright ridiculous. One method suggested I eat eight bananas and exercise for two to three hours every day to overcome anxiety! Although I understand the endless benefits of exercise, I didn't want it to consume my life. I also know the benefits of eating bananas, but if I ate eight a day I might have turned into one!

Asking you to complete unrealistic tasks is pointless, and I will never instruct you to do something that isn't well within your capability or that I haven't done myself. For me, it's about progress, not perfection. As long as I've got you on the right path and heading in the right direction, everything else is insignificant.

Humour

Overcoming anxiety and depression is a serious subject, and I never want to deflect attention away from that fact. However, I noticed that, when I suffered from anxiety and depression, I took things way too seriously, which severely damaged my ability to laugh at things, including myself.

Humour allows you to see things in a different light, which is why I like to add a healthy sprinkle of it. As you read the book, I expect you to laugh frequently. If you don't, I will of course be deeply offended.

Inspiration

Whether you draw inspiration from your own achievements, or the achievements of others, we all need to be inspired. I'm going to act as your friend, helping you confront and change your beliefs, and be as specific as I can be about my own experience, so you know exactly how I overcame anxiety and depression.

I want you to draw inspiration from the fact that I was in the same place you are now, and I know, without any doubt, change is possible. I don't have superhuman capabilities (I'm human, just like you), so you can do the same.

The difference

I wanted *Anxiety Rebalance* to be refreshingly different from other methods, due to the fact that nothing else helped me in the long term. I feel it's important to look at a few of the methods I used and highlight what I thought was good – and not so good.

Distraction

DISTRACTION ADVICE: Turn your music up, or do some other activity to take your mind off being anxious.

ME: OK, I did that, and for a while it did take my mind off being anxious – thanks a lot! But wait a minute... I'm starting to feel anxious again. What do I do now? Shall I keep distracting myself? How long do I have to keep doing it? A day? A week? A lifetime?

At this point, you can probably tell I'm not the biggest fan of distraction. I'm being polite – I actually think it's one of the worst solutions I've ever come across. Anybody that advocates it as a long-term solution for anxiety is either out to make a quick buck by misleading people, or they're going along with the masses, and therefore unaware of its ineffectiveness.

When my daughter falls over and hurts her knee, distraction is an excellent solution. To help her get over the short-term pain I distract her by picking her up and pretend to look for a cat (she loves cats), and that normally works. The short-term pain goes, and she forgets all about it – and that's the point I'm making: *short-term pain goes, but anxiety stays.*

Anxiety is well and truly implanted in us and, no matter how much we try and distract ourselves from it, it will always be there. The term itself is misleading – the word 'distraction' implies that you will always suffer from high anxiety, and the best you can do is distract yourself from it. This is not only uninspiring, but also completely untrue.

At best, distraction is a mask for symptoms, because it doesn't deal with the cause. This is fundamental to its ineffectiveness. Think of it like a house with damp. You can paint the walls to cover the damp so it looks nice but, left untreated, the damp will always come back, and probably worse than before. I was this house for ten years. I walked around with a painted face, living in denial and pretending that everything was going to be OK, until the inevitable damp set in again, and all it took was a small knock to bring the house down.

Not dealing with the root cause of anxiety is why most methods turn out to be ineffective. You'll keep doing them and doing them, expecting different results, but the end result will always be the same. That's why I'm such an advocate of talking therapies such as counselling – they help you get to the root cause of the issue and deal with it. Until you do that, it's hard to move forward.

Counselling | Therapy

I fully respect the work of counsellors and recommend counselling to anybody – with one stipulation: find a good one! You get good and bad in every profession, and over the years I looked for professional help in the form of counselling, I certainly saw a mixture of the two.

If you want to deal with your problems, including anxiety and depression, sharing and being able to communicate is absolutely crucial. When you need somebody impartial to talk to, an experienced counsellor is a great option. We haven't all got family or close friends we can go to, and counselling is sometimes the only option. You may not want to share your deepest thoughts and feelings with the people closest to you, so again, counselling is an ideal non-judgemental and impartial option.

I was fortunate enough to find a good counsellor who helped me rationalise my thoughts, giving my racing mind the comfort it needed. I also had some good support from a few friends and family, who offered me the tough love I needed to get me through the very rocky times. However, all of this combined still didn't solve the overall problem that was living inside me, and my theory on this is based on two fundamental reasons:

1. You have to deal with both your mindset *and* your lifestyle

Anxiety and depression need to be dealt with on two levels: mindset and lifestyle. Counselling can be effective in helping to change your mindset, but can fall short on lifestyle. You can only understand – and offer advice on – the changes you need to make in your lifestyle if you've lived it, breathed it, felt it, touched it, and been personally terrorised by it.

2. A lack of *true* understanding

I'm sure you agree that, unless you've personally experienced high anxiety and depression, it's hard to truly empathise with somebody who has. When it comes to dealing with it, there really is no substitute for personal experience. If you want to go down the path of revival, *true* knowledge will only come from somebody who's already been there.

If you can find a counsellor who has experienced anxiety and depression first-hand, you're normally on to a winner. They are more likely to understand that, along with tackling your mindset, lifestyle changes also need to take place for change to happen. The same goes for friends and family – if they've been through or understand an ounce of what you're going through, they're more likely to offer the support you need. This isn't always the case, however, and a sympathetic shoulder and sound advice might not be there and waiting. They aren't professionals, so I would always recommend seeing one, even if you have an abundance of support at home. For a long time I thought digging around in my past was a waste of time, but it turned out that there were a few skeletons in the closet that needed to be set free. With help from a good professional, that's what I did, and it formed a big part of my revival.

Hypnotherapy | Acupuncture

Hypnotherapy appealed to me when I was looking for a 'cure'. Who wouldn't want to shut their eyes and wake up without suffering from high anxiety? It was the perfect quick fix I was looking for. Sadly, it didn't turn out as I'd planned.

I went to see a counsellor who included hypnotherapy in her sessions. I was naturally sceptical, but at that stage if you'd told me putting my head in a vice for ten days would help, I would have tried it. I sat down in the chair and was asked to shut my eyes and allow my mind to drift off as she spoke softly and slowly, counting down from ten to one. We got to one, and I remember sitting there with my eyes closed, feeling as conscious as when I first walked in. Ten minutes went by, and there was still no change. My eyes were still closed, and she continued to ask me questions. I was politely answering, wondering how long we had left. I was too polite to stop the session, so it went on for the entire hour.

As I left, I wasn't entirely sure what I should have expected. I'd seen Paul McKenna's TV programmes, in which he got people to do silly things under hypnosis, so on that basis I suppose I was expecting more. I decided to write it off as a disappointing experience. Maybe hypnotherapy wasn't for me. Maybe it was the hypnotherapist, and if I tried somebody else, that might work? I decided to give it another go and found somebody with twenty years' experience... but got the same result. I suppose a lot of it depends on how receptive you are as a person. Translate that any way you like! I obviously wasn't receptive, and therefore hypnotism wasn't effective. However, I will continue to be open-minded, and if it works for you, who am I to tell you differently? If, like acupuncture, you find it a relaxing experience and a respite from the jaws of anxiety, why not continue it as part of your revival? It might well be one of the few things you do that relaxes you – so don't stop it. But you should remain aware that overcoming anxiety and depression also requires your full consciousness, with your eyes open – that's the only real way to deal with it.

Doctors | Medication

I'll start off by saying how much I respect doctors and the work they do. If I require medical assistance, they are the first people I call on. It's too easy to blame the medical world for the lack of effective help for anxiety and depression, so I don't blame doctors at all – I don't think it's as straightforward as that.

If you're experiencing mental health problems, your first point of call is normally your doctor. In a lot of cases you won't be going to your doctor knowing anxiety and/or depression is the cause of your problem, so it's up to your doctor to recognise and diagnose it. We'll all have unique experiences with anxiety and depression, and it can be linked to pretty much anything – which is why 50% of all cases your doctor will see are stress-related. Now, with this in mind, put yourself in the doctor's seat. It's a tough job. As a general practitioner (GP), their job is to know a little about a lot, and anxiety alone is a vast subject with many causes and symptoms.

Take breaking your leg, for example. If you break your leg, you break your leg. You put it in a cast and, given time, it mends. As you know, anxiety isn't that straightforward (unfortunately). Lots of things can be put down to anxiety and stress, and the complications caused by mental illness don't make your doctor's job easy. That's why medicines (including anti-depressants) are handed out as often as they are, without considering the long-term complications, including addiction. Things are progressively getting better, with the introduction of talk therapies, but there is still a long way to go.

'Taking an anti-depressant is like burning down the whole forest because one tree is diseased.'
- Ruby Wax

I was never a fan of taking medication. When I did, I thought it was the easy option. I'd take a pill and hope everything would be fine. The reality was, it's not that simple. I'm not ignorant, and recognise that, in a lot of cases of mental illness, prescription medication is required. However, I also see the argument for the other side – in many cases it's not needed and can safely be avoided. Dealing with a major trauma is very different from coping with everyday emotions, such as anxiety. Too many of us try to mask these emotions with medication, when this isn't the natural thing to do. We all go through turbulent times and should expect to experience sadness and anxiety as well as happiness and joy. They might hurt, but they are part of life. That's something we have to accept, not necessarily medicate.

Is medication a short-term solution for anxiety and depression? Maybe. I know I had times when my anxiety caused me so much pain I didn't think I had a choice. Anxiety and depression can make you hurt just as much as a physical pain, and our natural reaction to pain is to want to get rid of it. Sometimes that means taking medication/sedatives. Living in a developed country means we're lucky enough to have access to medicines, but you should always take prescription medication with the understanding that it isn't – and shouldn't be – a long-term solution, due to the complications it can cause, such as addiction. It's also worth noting that, in some cases, the side-effects are worse than the actual symptoms.

The longest I took medication for was three months, and I didn't get on with it at all (I'll tell you more about my experience later in the book). I was lucky not to develop a dependency on it, but I've met plenty of people who have, and some who have taken medication for years and now can't contemplate life without it. If you become dependent on drugs, then the thing that was supposed to help you ends up being the problem. When you're addicted and totally dependent on something, you can never be free, and that's why medication will never be a long-term solution for anxiety and depression. There's no freedom attached to being dependent on a pill. Freedom is part of overcoming anxiety and depression, and that means being able to break dependency. Relying on something else to ease your symptoms will lead you down a path you don't want to take.

I'm realistic enough to know that, whatever I say, or anybody else says, if you want to take medication, you're going to do it. If you do, I'd like you to think of it like the red and blue pill scene on the film *The Matrix.* (If you haven't seen it, I highly recommend it.)

In it, Morpheus gives Neo two options:

1. Take the blue pill and live in complete naivety. Nothing is real, but you'll never know it.

2. Take the red pill and discover the truth. Reality might be hard to take sometimes, but at least you won't be living a lie.

Like Neo, I chose the red pill.

The ethos

Having suffered for fifteen years from a condition that likes to overcomplicate everything, I'm a big fan of simplifying things. Let's use this theory and summarise how to deal with anxiety and depression. If you're overdue some good news, I have some for you here:

Dealing with anxiety and depression requires ONE thing:
BALANCE.

Picture a scale. On the left side you have anxiety, stress, fear, guilt, sadness and uncertainty. Look at the right side of the scale. It's empty. That scale is your life, and it's tipping way too much in one direction. You can't walk around in life lopsided! Not only will you look silly, but you'll soon topple over. You need to get BALANCE back in your life by counteracting the emotions on the left side and putting some weight on the right side using emotions like happiness, joy, love, excitement and certainty.

It's a simple enough theory – but then, all the best ones are. The funny thing about the simplest and best theories is that sometimes they're the hardest ones to spot and act on. When they are brought to the surface we're still too keen to follow everybody else, so we ignore the obvious, even if that means carrying on doing all the things that have never worked. We're too quick to doubt: 'Surely it can't be that easy?' I wrote this book to change this belief, because sometimes things really *are* that simple. If your life is filled with uncertainty, then you need more certainty to tip the balance. That's it. We may be embarrassed when we realise that things were never as bad as we imagined. Don't let pride get in your way. It's simple – sometimes as simple as making a different choice.

As well as accepting simplicity, we need to accept the fact that life is full of opposites: pleasure and pain, good and evil, love and hate. It has to work like that because life is far from perfect – it has to be imperfect and unbalanced to work! Whenever we have choice and freedom, anything can happen. As humans, we have plenty of both. It's part of our privilege and life's charm. Things are either going to go right or wrong, and feel good or bad. In a world where there's an abundance of happiness, love and joy, there will also be plenty of sadness, guilt and anxiety. In other words, you have to accept all of it, not just the good stuff. I don't mind admitting that I struggled with this concept for a long time. I overcomplicated everything. I blew everything out of proportion. As a people-pleaser, I couldn't cope with the idea that somebody might dislike me. That gave me a choice: accept it and move with it, or bury my head in the sand, close the door to the world, and become a recluse. No, no, no – I wasn't going to be defeated! I decided to open my door and accept the good *and* the bad; accept that I will have good and bad days, and anxiety will always be part of my life, in one form or another. Rather than fight nature, I decided I would work with it by getting my BALANCE right.

I'll quote Albert Einstein again here: *'Life is like riding a bicycle. To keep your balance, you must keep moving.'* That's so true. That doesn't mean you have to be ruthless to get on in life, though – far from it. What it does mean is you have to keep moving forward. If you stand still, locked in the same pattern of thoughts, doing the same thing you have always done, anxiety and depression will catch up with you. They will do the same thing they've always done to you – unless you keep moving forward and open your mind to change.

How to change

If you want to get on that bicycle and start moving your life forward, change is the one big thing that's needed. For me, change started when I understood what anxiety and depression were really about, including discovering the truth. *The truth about what?* I hear you ask. The truth that it's up to you what you do with your thoughts, and therefore, up to you how you choose to live. If you were to ask me where I draw my strength, it's from this knowledge. Knowing that it's my choice whether or not I let a thought ruin my day, or a pattern of thought destroy my future, has changed my life.

Before we get into all the other truths you need to know, there are a couple of things I want to cover:

1. You'll notice when I refer to anxiety I tend to call it *high* anxiety. I do this because levels of anxiety can be measured, and as a high-anxiety sufferer you're experiencing higher than normal levels of anxiety – that's it. The same principle applies when I refer to having low levels of energy – the lower the energy, the worse the depression.

2. You'll also notice that I tend to refer to anxiety more than I do depression (hence the title of the book). If you put yourself in the category of a depression sufferer rather than an anxiety sufferer, don't be alarmed: you've picked up the right book, I promise! Whether or not you're aware of it, if you have one, you have the other. Anxiety and depression go hand in hand, like strawberries and cream (without the nice taste).

In the simplest terms, high anxiety and depression are nothing more than a psychological IMBALANCE. The key to overcoming them is through knowing how to get your BALANCE right.

The truth about anxiety

There's no getting over the fact that high anxiety can be brutal, which is why our natural reaction is to fight against it. This is how we become quickly disillusioned; because it's a battle we'll *never* win. More importantly, it's a pointless battle we shouldn't be fighting in the first place.

'What you resist, persists.'
- Carl Jung

Anxiety is not your enemy. It's your life companion. It's essential to your survival, and if you didn't have it, you wouldn't be here today. By learning to live comfortably with it, and accepting it as part of your life, you will win – every time.

I'm continually shocked by the number of individuals who claim to be experts offering a 'cure' and 'elimination' for anxiety. It's difficult to understand how anybody with a *true* understanding of anxiety could make such false promises.

1. THERE IS *NO* CURE FOR ANXIETY (AND THERE NEVER WILL BE).

2. IT'S *IMPOSSIBLE* TO ELIMINATE ANXIETY.

It's no coincidence that I spent so many years looking for answers, and why people suffering from high anxiety are constantly seeking a 'cure'. It's because it doesn't exist!

Anxiety doesn't have a switch that you can permanently turn off. It's well and truly implanted in us and forms part of who we are, just like any other emotion. When we feel sad or angry, our natural reaction isn't to completely eliminate the emotions of sadness and anger – we accept them as part of our lives. We accept that it's healthy to get angry and upset. If we agree that it's healthy to get angry and sad, why are we led to believe that we should 'eliminate' anxiety, when it's just as healthy to be anxious? All of these emotions might come with unwanted and uncomfortable feelings, but that's part of the human experience. We would live in a very strange world if we felt happy every time we got dumped or fired, for example.

Anxiety is what gets you out of bed in the morning. It keeps you safe when you cross the road. It provides the motivation to find a loving partner and friends. It keeps your children fed and healthy. It makes your life possible. Save yourself a lot of grief and stop fighting it. Put your arm around it, and thank it for being a loyal companion.

How can you speak so fondly about something that destroyed your life for so long?

I now accept that anxiety will always be present in my life, and by changing its meaning, I completely change the way I deal with it. I understand that overcoming high anxiety is a life's journey, not a quick fix, and it's not something I can turn off, cure or eliminate.

Accepting anxiety as part of your life doesn't mean being ruled by it. The concept of rebalance means that once you've achieved normal anxiety levels you can live your life without having to make decisions based around it. You'll regain control, and be free to live a happy, active and fulfilling life, doing what you want, when you want.

The key to understanding why BALANCE is the only real solution to dealing with anxiety and depression is appreciating that *everybody* lives with it.

The only difference between a high-anxiety sufferer and somebody living a 'normal' life is how anxious they feel and for how long.

You really aren't alone, and that piece of information should give you all the reassurance you need to know that change is absolutely possible. No matter your background, how long you've experienced anxiety and depression, or the severity of your condition, *anyone* can achieve BALANCE.

WITH BALANCE, ANXIETY AND DEPRESSION WILL NEVER DICTATE YOUR LIFE AGAIN.

The Rebalance Scale™

What does BALANCE mean to you? How do you know when you've achieved it, and what's the end goal?

These are all important questions, and to help answer them I've put together the Rebalance Scale:

SCALE 7: Panic

SCALE 6: High anxiety

SCALE 5: Above-normal anxiety

SCALE 4: BALANCE

SCALE 3: Below-normal energy

SCALE 2: Low energy

SCALE 1: Sleep

SCALE 7: **Panic**

Panic – my best friend for many years! Obviously, I'm being sarcastic – there is nothing about panic that would ever make me class it as a friend. As a high-anxiety sufferer, I have no doubt you'll know all about it. You'll know that it sits at the top of the scale because it represents the most extreme form of anxiety and causes an array of unwanted symptoms, typically including sweating, dizziness, nausea, heart palpitations, shaking, numbness, tingling, chest pain and discomfort, loss of breath, a smothering or choking sensation, a dry mouth, a churning stomach, chills and hot flushes ... and any other symptom the mind can muster.

At the height of my high anxiety, panic attacks were a daily occurrence. Some were caused by obvious triggers, such as going to the supermarket. (The supermarket was a particular struggle for me, and always induced panic.) At other times, a panic attack would creep up on me without warning. I could be doing something as trivial as watching TV, when all of sudden I'd start to feel disorientated and uncomfortable. Because nothing obvious was causing these feelings, I'd panic because I didn't know what was going on.

It didn't matter how many times I experienced panic attacks and got through them, each time I was convinced there was something more sinister going on. I really believed I was ill and had a serious medical condition. It was incredibly frustrating. I'd plead with the doctor: 'Please diagnose me with something – anything – so I can stop this torment and move on.' But, as in so many other cases of panic, that diagnosis never came.

Examples of panic

- You regularly experience sharp bursts of panic created by anxious thoughts. These thoughts sometimes escalate into panic attacks, which can last for varying periods of time.

- You're able to recognise why you feel panicky (for example, being in a place that makes you feel uncomfortable), but you're not always sure.

- Panic can be sporadic and unpredictable, sometimes creeping up on you when you least expect it. For example, while driving you start to feel a smothering sensation, which causes a panic attack.

- Symptoms of panic (most likely chest pain) cause you to fear for your life and seek emergency medical assistance.

- You regularly feel the urge to get away from a situation and retreat to your 'safe place'.

- You avoid certain situations and places where you have previously panicked, such as a supermarket or restaurant.

- When you experience panic you sometimes feel like you are an observer, detached from your environment, looking on with a sense of unreality.

- Panic sometimes makes you feel like you're 'going mad', and the thought of losing control scares you.

SCALE 6: **High anxiety**

High anxiety is best explained using the analogy of a swimming duck. Everything above water (on the outside) might appear calm, but underneath the water (on the inside) you're frantically paddling, trying to hold things together. I spent most of the fifteen years I suffered living like this. I'd be sitting on my sofa watching TV, yet feel like I was at war on the frontline. From opening my eyes in the morning to going to bed at night, high anxiety ruled my life, and all my decisions were based around it.

Examples of high anxiety

- You avoid crowded places such as supermarkets, because they make you feel light-headed, dizzy, disorientated, or as if you might faint.
- You don't like to be left alone and have developed a dependency on somebody close to you (a partner, friend or family member).
- You like to be in control of everything in your life.
- You pay attention to your health and exaggerate symptoms: you think a headache might be a brain tumour, and chest pain could mean you're going to have a heart attack.
- You're often ill and prone to illness, suffering from aches, pains, headaches and numbness in certain areas of your body, including the chest, neck and back.

- You're picky about what you eat and drink because you're conscious about how different foods make you feel.
- You regularly suffer from digestion issues, including indigestion and stomach cramps.
- You search symptoms on the internet and visit the doctor seeking reassurance.
- You sometimes feel fearful for no reason, overwhelmed and unable to cope.
- You suffer from sleep deprivation and struggle to fall asleep at night due to not being able to switch off the thoughts racing through your mind.
- You have nightmares, and often wake up in the middle of the night (sometimes with chills).
- You feel physically and emotionally drained.
- You have a 'safe place' – typically your home – and have a radius within which you're willing to travel, feeling uncomfortable when you're too far away. Whenever you feel highly anxious, you seek relief by returning to your safe place.
- You fear the outside world and prefer to stay at home. This might lead to becoming housebound (agoraphobic).
- You are sometimes plagued by feelings of dread.
- You feel on edge and uncomfortable in a social environment.
- You turn down social opportunities and are absent at significant events (such as weddings), which affects your friendships and relationships.

- You're highly self-conscious and sometimes paranoid about what other people think of you.

- You experience obsessive thoughts and have set routines. For example, you won't leave your house or go on a trip without taking a certain drink or an object you depend on (such as a mobile phone), or you may have to check several times that your front door is locked when you leave your house.

SCALE 5: **Above-normal anxiety**

These symptoms are similar to those of high anxiety, but are less pervasive. You're able to operate and cope in everyday life without anxiety dominating your decisions, but it still plays its part, manifesting itself through mild forms of anxiety-related disorders.

Examples of above-normal anxiety

- You're snappy, short-tempered and easily aggravated.
- You sometimes vent your frustration and anger on the people closest to you, including your partner and children.
- You take the stress of your job home with you.
- Small things you never paid attention to previously and could dismiss now bother you. For example, if somebody is critical of you, it will affect your mood.
- Thoughts play on your mind and you focus on problems, rather than good things in your life. You may worry a lot about the future and everything on your to-do list.
- You're indecisive, and don't like to commit to something and risk that it might go wrong.

- You drink a little more alcohol than usual, and use it to help you relax.

- You find it difficult to concentrate and remember things.

- You consciously make the decision to avoid crowded places, such as supermarkets and shopping centres, or visit them at their quietest periods.

- You're easily alarmed or frightened.

- You find yourself turning down social opportunities more frequently, and view them as an inconvenience rather than a positive experience, preferring to stay at home.

- Your sleep pattern is affected by worry, and you often find it hard to fall asleep.

SCALE 4: **BALANCE**

Sitting comfortably within normal levels of anxiety and energy, BALANCE is the optimal place to be. You're living an active and healthy lifestyle without anxiety and depression dictating your decisions and actions. Anxiety isn't present in your immediate thoughts, and it only presents itself when genuinely needed. Until then, it sits quietly as your life companion, keeping you away from danger and helping you make sensible decisions (doing its job properly). You don't feel tired or drained, and have enough mental and physical energy to cope with life's usual daily challenges.

It's likely you'll be able to recall a time you felt like this, but if it's been a while, let me remind you what it feels like.

What BALANCE feels like

- You look forward to going out with friends, rather than counting down the days in dread.

- You can do the simple things in life (like going to the shop for some milk) without thinking about them.

- Going out for a nice meal with your partner doesn't create endless 'what if...?' thoughts that generate gut-wrenching apprehension and worry.

- An 'off day' is exactly that, and whenever you experience one you accept that everybody has them and move on to the next day. It doesn't mean your world is about to cave in: it was just a bad day, and tomorrow is another day.

- You can go to a friend's wedding without feeling ill or having to make excuses for being absent.
- A family holiday means enjoyment, relaxation and a well-deserved break.
- You're confident and feel good about yourself.
- Butterflies in your stomach mean happiness, surprise and excitement – not panic.
- Obsessive and overwhelming thoughts are replaced by healthy focus and ambition.
- Small things stay small, and don't snowball into big unwieldy troubles. Problems can be broken down and dealt with.
- Being stuck in traffic doesn't create uncontrollable rage and panic.
- Your outlook on life is objective and you're open-minded. Your immediate view isn't negative.
- You feel content and grateful for everything you have.
- You fall asleep easily when your head hits the pillow, and you wake up feeling energised and refreshed.
- The future is bright, and there's plenty to look forward to.

Most importantly, BALANCE means FREEDOM. No hang-ups, no emotional ties, no psychological baggage – just you, living how you want to live.

SCALE 3: **Below-normal energy**

Because anxiety goes hand in hand with depression, it's present at both ends of the scale. It will zap your positivity and happiness, and work with depression to lower your energy. The lower your energy, the greater your depression. Scale 3 represents lower than normal energy, which could be the early signs of a deeper depression.

Examples of below-normal energy

- You feel lethargic and more tired than usual.
- You don't feel as happy as the people around you.
- You're unmotivated, uninspired, and lack drive and passion.
- You're cynical, and when you talk about people you pick fault with them.
- You don't feel content, and think about how unsatisfied you are with your life.
- You regularly think about how you're feeling – in a negative way.
- You don't feel good about yourself, and have little interest in activities and socialising.

- You often blame yourself for things out of your control, and feel guilty, even if things aren't your fault.

- You have less time for romance, and regularly have low libido/little interest in sex.

- Happiness doesn't come as easily to you as it did previously.

- You prefer not to think about the future.

SCALE 2: **Low energy**

Scale 2 represents a deeper anxiety-induced depression and a lower level of unhappiness; you experience the same symptoms as with below-normal energy, but to a greater extent.

Examples of low energy

- You struggle to get out of bed in the morning, and lack the motivation and energy to do even the most trivial daily task.
- You don't want to face the world, and feel detached from it.
- You would rather stay at home with the curtains drawn than face the prospect of going out to meet people.
- You feel restless, agitated and impatient.
- You can't be bothered to shower or wash, and your personal hygiene suffers.
- You have a poor appetite, which means you regularly skip meals – or you may binge on unhealthy foods.
- Life feels as though it's slowing down.
- You're easily tearful and often cry.

- You have low self-esteem and confidence, and when you look in the mirror you don't feel good about yourself.

- You find it hard to get rid of a feeling of despair.

- You regularly ask yourself, 'What's the point?'

- You spend long periods resting or sleeping.

- You read SCALE 4 (BALANCE) and thought being happy and free was impossible and unachievable.

SCALE 1: **Sleep**

At the very bottom of the scale, sleep represents extreme depression, just as panic represents an extreme form of anxiety. I went through long periods of both. When I was deeply depressed, all I wanted to do was sleep all day. It felt as though my body was shutting down (like when you reboot your computer), and sleep was my only escape from the clutches of anxiety. On average, I would sleep sixteen hours a day – twice as long as the average adult needs. In the few hours I was awake, anxiety had a way of sucking any remaining bit of life out of me. My energy became non-existent, and I felt mentally and physically exhausted every waking second of every day. It made breaking the anxiety and depression cycle very difficult, because all I wanted to do was (you guessed it) sleep more.

At the other extreme, sleep deprivation (caused by high anxiety) was the worst symptom I experienced. I know exactly what it feels like to be a zombie on *The Walking Dead*. Three days of not sleeping properly, red-eyed with dribble running down my chin, unable to talk, was as bad as it got for me. This is a typical example of the continuous rigmarole I went through on a nightly basis:

As soon as my head hit the pillow I have racing thoughts about all the bills that need to be paid this month and the work I have left to do. I'm exhausted, but it doesn't matter how tired I am, I just can't fall asleep. I lie there with my eyes wide open, just staring at the ceiling, until I'm so frustrated I decide to get up. I make myself a drink. I know going back to bed will be a waste of time so I lie down on the couch and put the television on. It keeps me company so I don't feel so alone.

My eyes are heavy. I look at the clock. It's the early hours of the morning and I start to panic – I'm desperate to sleep because I know I'm going to feel like a zombie at work the next day.

Eventually, panic subsides, and through pure exhaustion I fall asleep at around 4am. After a few hours I wake up on the couch, feeling like I haven't slept at all. I immediately start to feel anxious, and I'm already worrying about how I'm going to get through the day.

I dread going to bed because I know it's all going to happen again.

Eventually, with time and practice, I sorted my sleep out. If I hadn't done this, I had no chance of overcoming anxiety and depression. That's why I can't stress enough how important it is to get it right. A strong pattern of sleep combined with the ability to relax is essential for achieving BALANCE.

If sleep is a problem for you (and I'm guessing it is), rest assured – we'll look at how to combat it within Part 4, Ten Actions to Achieve BALANCE.

Achieving BALANCE

I read the examples on all the seven scales and could relate to most of them. Is this normal?

It's completely normal to identify with most of the examples at both ends of the scale. Life is a balancing act, and we're all trying to stay on the rope! The things in life that cause you to fall (or, of course, support you along the way), and influence how you feel at any one time, typically include mood, relationships, health, stress and environment, making it perfectly natural to experience emotional change on a regular basis. Life is unpredictable, and the only way to deal with its inevitable ups and downs is to appreciate that fact. You can only deal with the emotions it brings through achieving BALANCE.

The Rebalance Scale is designed to help you recognise the various stages of anxiety and depression, and give a clearer picture of how to achieve BALANCE. The two main ingredients that bind it all together, and make achieving BALANCE possible, are *practice* and *time*.

Practice

You might not view it this way, but for however long you've suffered from anxiety, you've been practising how to do it – and you've probably become very good at it. You've become accustomed to the life you're living now, and your brain thinks it's the right way to live, when you and I know it's not.

Your 'comfort zone' is being formed daily by what you're practising, and if you're suffering from anxiety and depression, it's likely to be shrinking. The little world you're allowed to live in is keeping you alive and away from danger (well, that's what your brain is telling you). Yes, the smaller your world, the safer you are, might be true, but if you're too scared to leave your house then this is a real problem.

We all have our own comfort zones and perceive things in different ways. What would your immediate reaction be if I invited you to come skydiving with me tomorrow? Some of you might be thrilled with the invite, but some of you might have thrown this book across the room in hysteria simply at the thought of doing it. It's an extreme example, but as a high-anxiety sufferer, you will have very little tolerance of risk. As your comfort zone keeps shrinking, you'll do less and less, especially if that means you jumping out of a plane.

High anxiety and depression also take over your rational thought, and they take your comfort zone with it. They want your comfort zone to be as tiny as possible, because that makes the job of keeping you alive and safe much easier. They would rather you stay at home locked up in your bedroom than face the big bad world. Because of this shrinking comfort zone, the things you used to do that were once second nature to you become frightening and unachievable: for example, going on holiday. It's no longer the relaxing and refreshing break from the stresses of work and life it should be – it's a terrifying, panic-inducing nightmare. From the moment the booking is confirmed, your thoughts turn into psychological warfare.

'What if I panic on the plane? What if the plane crashes?'

'What if something bad happens while I'm away? What if we're burgled?'

'What if I hate the hotel and I can't get home?'

The more you worry and think about what *might* happen, the more you avoid going on holiday, and the more you avoid going on holiday, the more you're *practising* how to avoid things, and the less likely you are to ever want to go on holiday again. The comfort zone shrinking process starts with you avoiding going on holiday (leaving the country), and it then shrinks further until you avoid leaving a certain radius of your 'safe place' (normally your home), until you become so agoraphobic that going to the shop becomes unbearable. Now you can see how quickly something as simple as getting a pint of milk can turn into a problem. The comfort zone of survival is tightened so much that life becomes totally unrealistic, even for the most rational person, and you keep practising how to do it.

So, how does this relate to achieving BALANCE? You have to start practising the life you want, rather than living and practising the life you *don't* want. Achieving BALANCE requires you to retrain your brain, and practice is the only way you can do it. Have you ever asked somebody, 'Are you nervous?' and they've answered, 'No, I've done this hundreds of times before'? Practice increases confidence and familiarity, and the more you practise being a balanced person, the easier it will become, until it becomes second nature again.

Time

Time is just as significant as practice. I will challenge anybody who says they were instantly 'cured' of high anxiety and depression. It's impossible to change the bad habits of a mental health condition in an instant. Your brain is following the pattern you've created, and it takes time to break that pattern. Your brain needs to learn the new one. It's like saying you can learn a new language in an instant.

What is absolutely possible is *creating instant change* – changing what and how you believe in something. If you recognise, and make an effort to stop following, the same pattern, instant change can arise from that, including an immediate reduction in anxiety and a massive increase in energy. If you want to keep breaking the pattern it will take time and practice to get good at it, until you become a pro. Like learning a new language, some people will take to it like a duck in water, some will struggle a little but keep going, and some will quit.

Time is also significant because it plays a part in how deeply rooted the habit is in your brain. Usually, the longer you've suffered, the harder it is to break the habit. If you've suffered from anxiety and depression for many years, you'll have to work harder to overcome it than somebody who has suffered for a few months. If you take another look at the scale, you'll see that issues normally arise when sustained periods of time are spent at either end of the scale. For example, a high-anxiety sufferer will spend most of their time between 5 and 7 on the scale:

SCALE 7: Panic
SCALE 6: High anxiety
SCALE 5: Above-normal anxiety

If you're living with anxiety-induced depression, you'll spend most of your time between 1 and 3:

SCALE 3: Below-normal energy
SCALE 2: Low energy
SCALE 1: Sleep

When I suffered from high anxiety and depression, I spent long periods of time at both ends of the scale. It was also common for me to experience the entire scale on a daily basis. I could wake up in panic (7), which was quickly followed by feelings of desperation and depression, making me want to throw the blanket over my head and go back to sleep (1).

The reason you are where you are right now is down to time and practice. These two things have dictated your current position and mindset. So far they've worked more against you than for you, and that's something you need to change.

The stages of anxiety and depression

If you lost your keys and had a moment of panic, would you say you suffer from high anxiety? What if, all day, every day, for two months, you experienced the same feeling of panic you get when you lose your keys, but without any real reason or explanation? It's a simple and straightforward point, but it's one that's lost on most anxiety and depression sufferers. It's easy to forget that your condition has got to the stage it has due to *time*.

Think about it. If you lose your keys, a moment of panic is normal. If you still can't find your keys after a few hours of searching, it's normal to experience more anxiety until you either find them or you get another set. It's only when you experience consistent anxiety following the event that it becomes an issue, especially when there's no good or apparent reason. The same thing goes for depression. If you left your favourite jacket on the train, it's normal to feel down for a few hours (maybe even a few days). It's only when you continue to feel depressed over a lengthier period of time that it becomes an issue.

Losing your keys or jacket isn't life-changing, so the severity of the event also plays its part. You can normally pinpoint the trigger of a condition (such as panic disorder) to a significant life event or trauma (such as bereavement), but it's not always that straightforward, and it could start from anything, big or small. Whatever it starts from, time is the key.

How long is it before anxiety and depression become an issue for me?

Only you can answer that. For some, having a day full of anxiety can lead to further issues, whereas others might only start to experience long-term issues following a much lengthier spell of stress.

I started to notice issues in my early teens, when I began to worry about things that didn't exist, and the 'what if...' scenarios took over. These thoughts got progressively worse following my first panic attack (at the age of sixteen). I started to fear having another, and that fuelled my anxiety further. Before I knew it, ten more years of suffering had gone by. Does this make me weak or stupid? Should I have done something about it earlier? I think it would be harsh to think so, especially considering how easy it is to stick with the same routine, rather than make a change. The fear of change can make the clock go by very quickly.

To show you how easy it can be to jump from dealing with a stressful time to living a life controlled by high anxiety and depression, I've highlighted the following four stages using a typical example.

Stage 1
You're dealing with a particularly stressful time at work, your bills are getting on top of you, and you're trying to deal with family issues. Your stress levels are higher than usual, and you begin to experience symptoms above the normal level of anxiety (Scale 5). These symptoms are a natural reaction to stress, but they get progressively worse because you find it difficult to cope.

Stage 2
A few days go by and you wonder how you're going to survive. More bills come through the letterbox, and debt collectors are demanding money. Your child is suspended from school for fighting, and your boss wants to see you about the deadlines you keep missing. Symptoms of high anxiety (Scale 6) develop, and you experience your first panic attack at work (Scale 7).

Stage 3
The next day you call in sick because you're worried about having another panic attack. Worry plagues your mind and you begin to feel more lethargic than usual (Scale 3). A few more days of staying at home worrying make you feel more depressed, and you start to wonder what the point is of getting out of bed in the morning (Scale 2). You'd rather sleep all day than face reality (Scale 1).

Stage 4
A few more days go by, and you're now coping rather than living. Thoughts like 'how am I going to pay the bills if I'm not at work?', 'what if I get fired?', 'what if I lose my house?' and 'how will I support my family?' buzz around in your head constantly. High anxiety and depression are now firmly part of your life, dictating how and where you live your life. The weeks, months and years go by, with you continuing to experience symptoms from scales 1–7. Decades go by, and you look back on your life, wondering how you've dealt with such a debilitating condition for so long.

Because we're all unique, there will of course be many variations to this, but the development of the condition generally follows the same pattern: practised habitual behaviour that progressively gets worse as time passes.

How long will it take me to achieve BALANCE?

Habits can be broken within seconds, but that's the wrong question to ask. At this stage it's more important you know that achieving BALANCE is a life's journey, not a quick fix. If you were released from prison following a lengthy sentence, would you expect to comfortably integrate back into society straightaway? Anxiety and depression have shackled your brain, and it takes time to break the habit, appreciate freedom and achieve BALANCE, just like time played a factor in the development of your condition.

I'm still learning today, and the learning never ends. The journey will have its ups and downs, but the stronger your belief in change, the more likely it will be that the ups will be much more frequent than the downs. When that's the case, BALANCE will be much easier to sustain. As long as you keep following my advice and put the effort in, the journey will feel much more like business class, rather than a donkey ride along a rickety road.

The four parts of *Anxiety Rebalance*

The following four parts have been placed in the correct order, which is why I encourage you to take them one step at a time, making sure you master each step before moving on. More impatient people (like me) will probably complete the book in a few sittings. If that's the case, be sure to check back and use the information as a reference. Whatever your style, just make sure you feel confident that you have thoroughly covered each part before moving on. They are all essential, and you won't achieve BALANCE without them.

Part 1: Anxiety Exposed

Part 1 is about exposing anxiety for what it *really* is by shining a big light on it. Once it's been exposed and has nowhere to hide, you can move from the passenger seat to the driver's seat, and be ready to take back control.

Part 2: Techniques to Reduce Anxiety and Increase Energy

Part 2 includes all the techniques that helped me reduce my anxiety and increase my energy. When your anxiety is reduced and your depression is lifted, you'll start to feel immediate benefits. Anxiety won't dominate your thinking, and you'll be ready to start looking at your future and make changes.

Part 3: Realign Your Focus

Your focus dictates where your life is going, and if you are focusing on anxiety and depression, there are no prizes for guessing where you'll end up. I've designed Part 3 to realign your focus, and help steer you in the direction you want your future to go. When you're heading in the right direction, you're ready to find out what it takes to achieve and sustain BALANCE.

Part 4: Ten Actions to Achieve BALANCE

The final part includes the ten actions you need to take to achieve and sustain BALANCE. Achieving and sustaining BALANCE is a better solution than simply going back to the time when your condition didn't exist. Through education and guidance I'm offering the chance of *real* lifetime freedom, and by following these ten actions, you will make sure your journey continues and you stay on an even keel.

PART 1:
ANXIETY EXPOSED

Fight or flight – an abused system

You've probably heard of the 'fight or flight' reaction. It's a marvellous tool to get us out of real or perceived situations of danger. If you're interested in knowing how it works, there's plenty of information you can find on the subject. For those of you more interested in knowing how we completely misuse and abuse this bodily reaction, why it causes uncontrollable anxiety, and what we can do to stop it, let me sum it up...

Example

Imagine you're in bed and you hear a noise downstairs. You instantly become alert as your sound receptors acutely tune into the noise. As you listen, you hear a door being opened and heavy footsteps walking across the kitchen floor. Your suspicions are confirmed: there is somebody in your house. Your fight or flight system is instantly activated and adrenaline is pumped into your body, causing a cocktail of reactions:

- Your body shuts down non-essential systems, including digestion and the immune system, to boost your energy.
- Your heart rate rises and blood pressure shoots up, rushing blood to the major muscle groups.
- Oxygen is pumped into your lungs.
- Your muscles are fuelled with adrenaline and glucose, ready for danger.
- Your pupils dilate to let in as much light as possible.

- You focus intensely on the present danger, and everything else becomes insignificant.

In this example, when facing a potential burglar, the fight or flight response is perfectly rational and acceptable. All of these reactions are designed to give you the speed, strength and alertness you need to deal with a threat. However, what if there is no burglar? What if, after the event, you find yourself staying awake every night expecting to be burgled? What if you're unable to relax, and feel constantly uneasy at home? You've become oversensitive, and now you're abusing your fight or flight system.

Being oversensitive

If you experience a burglary, the possibility of you being burgled again is now on your mind, making you more sensitive to it (compared to somebody who has never been burgled). If you add to this the fact that a highly anxious brain is very impressionable, something like a burglary can be the catalyst to a rocky road full of anxiety. It's like opening Pandora's Box – once you experience something, your mind is open to it, taking it from the unknown to reality.

Take millionaires, for example. There are lots of examples of millionaires losing and regaining their wealth many times over. To them, making millions is a reality, so when they lose it they know they can make it back again, because they've done it before.

How does this relate to anxiety?

If you've experienced anxiety and/or panic attacks your mind is now open to the prospect, making it a reality. It wasn't *real* until you experienced it. It suddenly went from something you might have heard about to something that is taking over your life. With the reality now firmly implanted in your mind, anxiety and panic can and will influence your decisions, and if it becomes overwhelming (as it can easily do), generalised anxiety disorder (GAD) can quickly become part of your life.

Different people deal with traumatic events (like a burglary) in different ways. How you will deal with it depends on the severity of the event and your mental wellbeing. A balanced person with strong mental wellbeing will consider the fact that burglary happens all the time, and although it was a distressing event, they won't let it cause any further anguish. They will naturally be sensitive to it, but won't allow feelings of vulnerability to lead to panic and further anxiety. To somebody in a state of high anxiety, seeing a story about a burglary in the newspaper might be all it takes to trigger the fight or fight response, or it might activate simply by mentioning the word 'burglary'. This is because the brain has put great emphasis on a burglary being a threat to their survival, and a *big* spotlight is shone on anything related to it.

BURGLARY = THREAT TO SURVIVAL = FIGHT OR FLIGHT

How long you suffer after the event, again, depends on its severity and your mental wellbeing. Feelings of high anxiety are felt the most after the event due to it being fresh in your mind. As time passes, the memory will fade (time really is a great healer). In the case of a burglary, it's likely you'll check window and door locks multiple times before you go to bed. Apprehension creates tension, and keeps you on high alert in case it happens again, so you might also find it hard to fall asleep, and feel a little uneasy in your home. The reason behind all these thoughts and feelings (whatever the period of time) always comes back to the perception of something being a threat to your survival. Trauma will always cause anxiety, even for the healthiest mind, and that can last for days, weeks or – in rare cases of post-traumatic stress disorder (PTSD) – sometimes a lot longer.

It's also important to factor in the place where trauma is experienced, because that can also play a big part in how you handle things in future. For example, if you experienced a panic attack in a supermarket it's likely you'll avoid the supermarket because your brain has associated it with a threat to your survival. If you continue to avoid the supermarket, you'll find it harder to set foot in one again. Unfortunately, your brain won't stop there. If you let it, it will continue to associate all public places (being outside or away from your comfort zone) with a threat to your survival, which can lead to suffering from panic attacks in all public places, until eventually you're too scared to leave your house entirely (agoraphobia). Given lots more time, with anxiety and depression hitting hard, this will be just the beginning of your problems. There won't be a shortage of anxiety-related disorders ready to pounce, OCD being just one of them. If we go back to the burglary example, to try and control your feelings you might develop OCD by checking locks, windows and doors a certain number of times. If you don't check them the set amount of times you've told yourself is acceptable (five times, for example), you will convince yourself you'll be burgled again, which will put you in a constant state of alert. Can you now see how this can very quickly spiral out of control? It's pure torture and self-abuse, not to mention exhausting!

If anxiety is left to spiral out of control it will continue to abuse the fight or flight system, which will inevitably lead to further irrational fears and disorders, causing you to overthink everything. Overthinking creates problems that don't exist, and these irrational and constant thoughts result in the world of 'what if...?'

The world of 'what if...?'

Welcome to the world of high anxiety – or, as I call it, the world of 'what if...?'

I lived in this world for a long time. It wasn't a nice place. The constant feeling of paranoia was overwhelming, and everywhere I went people were out to get me. *Why is that person looking at me? Is there something wrong with me?* I lost count of the number of times I had unspeakable things happen to me, how many times I died a horrible death, and the number of disasters that took place – in my mind, of course.

The first memory I have of living in the world of 'what if...?' was in my early teens. I would overthink and worry about everything, including the smallest details, with my thoughts generally negative and totally irrational. High anxiety kept me believing that every event would lead to an unpleasant or disastrous outcome, and this became more real every day, including the belief that a headache must be a brain tumour, and a bit of chest pain must mean I was about to have a heart attack. However, if I'd written down each fearful thought I had each day, I would have seen that the vast majority, if not all of them, didn't actually happen. Try it and see for yourself. From the moment you wake up, write down all the negative thoughts you have and see how many actually happen. Most of them won't, because they're based on fearful 'what if...' scenarios that are irrational and, quite frankly, pointless. The only purpose they serve is to drain you, and take the little energy you have away.

I openly admit that most of the thoughts I had were irrational and pointless, but that didn't stop the continuous flow. They were very difficult to control – worrying about what *might* happen was a daily routine. When you add the OCD rituals to the equation (which are an attempt to try and control these thoughts) it made it even more unbearably tiring. As my thoughts became more and more irrational, channels of possibility were opened in my brain that exceeded the realms of rational thought. Each irrational thought laid another brick on the labyrinth that was being constructed in my mind, making me feel trapped and unable to escape. When I tried to take another route there was always an irrational and pointless thought ready to put up its brick wall and prevent my escape.

I allowed this cycle of stress and worry to continue, and my 'what if...' beliefs become more extreme and frequent, until my life was completely dictated by them. I'd worry and stress about the smallest things, and my nerves were constantly on edge. The door would knock or the phone would ring and I'd jump out of my skin. Something as insignificant as spilling a drink on the floor created panic in me. 'What if...' anxious thoughts became an addiction and, like any addiction, they became very hard to stop. My extended abuse of the fight or flight system and constant 'what if...' thoughts inevitably resulted in me being trapped in the fear cycle.

The fear cycle

Being trapped in the fear cycle will seriously cloud your judgement and ability to think rationally. Take chest pain, for example. To a balanced person, a pain in the chest area could be due to indigestion or some other rational reason, and they will happily go about their day without concern. A high-anxiety sufferer, who is already hypersensitive to all bodily feelings, will associate the pain with a heart problem (most likely a heart attack) and will think their life is in danger, triggering the fight or flight response. Adrenaline will surge around their body, causing heart palpitations, sweating, breathlessness, dizziness and imaginary pains associated with a heart attack that they have read about (such as pains down the arm), all of which reinforce the fact that they're having a heart attack and might die. The reality is that their life is not in danger, and rather than the adrenaline being used for a genuine life or death scenario, it's used to fuel more 'what if...' thoughts.

'What if I need an ambulance?'

'What if it's not a heart attack and I'm over-reacting? I'll be embarrassed.'

'What if it is a heart attack? I might die!'

These thoughts prolong the panic, and if they cause a panic attack, it will continue as long as the fear cycle continues.

FEAR = FIGHT OR FLIGHT = ADRENALINE = FEAR = ADRENALINE = FEAR = ADRENALINE = FEAR...

The cycle will eventually come to an end: it always does. The timescale is dependent on the circumstances and thought process. In a prolonged panic attack, your body won't have enough energy to continue the cycle, so it will normally end due to exhaustion.

There are less extreme versions of the fear cycle, like with GAD, where someone experiences a constant feeling of anxiety. Whatever the example, whether fear is extreme or constant, short-lived or long-lasting, the fear cycle is to blame. You can only break it by getting out of it, and getting out of it requires you to understand why you're in it.

Fearing the fear

At the peak of my highly anxious state I suffered from a constant dull pain in my chest area. I was aware of it day and night, and always worried about it. The uncertainty about what was causing it overwhelmed me, and I focused on it all the time. The more I focused on it and tried to fight it, the worse it became. I was convinced there was something wrong with my heart. No matter how many tests I had (all of which came back clear), or the amount of reassurance given by medical professionals, nothing put my mind at ease.

It wasn't like any other pain. When I twisted my ankle playing badminton, I fully expected it to hurt for a few weeks. I accepted the pain as 'normal' and didn't attach any uncertainty to it. I couldn't accept the dull pain in my chest in the same way because I didn't know what it was. If I didn't know what it was, how could I accept it? It was 'abnormal' and the not knowing sent me crazy. My only option was to put up with it – I felt as though I had to accept it as part of my life or risk going insane. It was there and it was constant, and the only way I could deal with it was to suppress it as much as I could.

I now know that if I'd dealt with the thoughts connected to it and not detached it from emotion, I could have dealt with it a lot sooner. So why didn't I do it sooner? Why did I allow it to live me with me for so many years? Was I afraid to confront it? Did I accept it as part of my habitual behaviour? Yes. Looking back, it's clear to me now that I was too scared to confront it, so I just let it exist.

Confronting and dealing with it has allowed me to find out exactly what its cause was. I know a lot of people can relate to persistent 'abnormal' symptoms, so I'm pleased to be able to give you the answer:

I WAS LIVING INSIDE THE FEAR CYCLE, AND FEARED THE FEAR.

You can call it apprehension, uncertainty, or the unknown if you like, but I feared what fear might do next, which caused my constant feeling of anxiousness. This was then manifested as a symptom – for me, the dull pain in my chest.

The fear itself becomes the overwhelming issue, and will continue for however long you fear the fear. Anxiety is no longer just the thing that makes you nervous before an audition, job interview or driving test. It's constantly there, playing on your mind, and the feeling of apprehension eats away at you and affects every aspect of your life. Uncertainty makes you afraid to leave your house, and the unknown keeps you awake at night.

Whatever the effects and symptoms you experience, it's likely they exist because you fear the fear.

Anxiety on the mind

Imagine your mind is a planet and your worrying thoughts are the little people who live on your planet. As the creator, is it not up to you how many of these little people live on your planet, what significance they hold, or if they exist at all? The existence of high anxiety is dictated by your mind.

'The mind is everything. What you think, you become.'
– Buddha

It's a habit

Have you ever formed an opinion about somebody, only to be proved completely wrong, or change your mind once you've actually spoken to him? You based that first opinion on learned (habitual) behaviour and what you perceive to be right. We make our minds up very quickly and instinctively. Sometimes we're right, sometimes we're wrong. The thing influencing our decision is habit, and the more we do it, the more habits are formed.

Depending on the length of time you've suffered from anxiety, your brain has been conditioned to think the way it does – the longer the time, the stronger the conditioning.

'We are what we repeatedly do.'
- Aristotle

Take smoking, for example. A smoker will become addicted to nicotine, and throughout the day all they can think of is their next cigarette break. (I smoked for fifteen years and can vouch for this.) The longer they've smoked, the stronger the habit/addiction. Now replace a cigarette with an anxious thought, and you'll understand how high anxiety is a habit, just like smoking.

It's normal for anxiety to be part of our decision-making process, but when 'what if...' thoughts consistently hound you, anxiety can quickly become a habit, until it feels abnormal not to worry. **Just like any other bad habit, high anxiety can be stopped.** We can crush those addictive irrational thoughts just as easily as stamping out a cigarette on the floor.

Anxiety works on two levels, consciously and subconsciously. Before I explain this further, I need to quickly highlight the difference between the two.

Conscious mind
If you took a bite out of an apple, your conscious mind has governed that action because you were consciously aware that you did it.

Subconscious mind
The subconscious mind is responsible for all the actions you do which you aren't aware of, like breathing and blinking. If you intentionally took control of your breathing or blinking, it would be your conscious mind taking over.

This is very straightforward, but being aware of the difference between the two is significant when it comes to overcoming anxiety and depression. I explain it best using my 'autopilot' theory.

Autopilot

It's a fact that high-anxiety sufferers have fewer car accidents. There are positives and negatives attached to this fact. The positives are obvious. The negative is you never allow yourself to switch off, or allow your brain to switch to autopilot.

When I refer to your 'autopilot', I'm referring to your subconscious mind.

Can you remember a time when you were driving and couldn't remember how you reached your destination? You were so consumed by various thoughts that you weren't consciously paying attention to your driving. This is because your subconscious mind (autopilot) kicked in. Driving was second nature to you, so your brain felt comfortable enough to put your autopilot in charge. The same applies to all tasks you're familiar with, particularly easy ones. When you watch TV or clean the house you don't need all your brainpower, so it's natural for your brain to go into autopilot. It makes doing mundane and boring jobs more bearable.

When a pilot needs a rest, she has the option to switch to autopilot or ask her co-pilot to take over when required. The pilot can't be expected to be on constant full alert for the whole journey, especially if it's a long one. The brainpower needed for that is exhausting, and it's likely the passengers wouldn't get on the plane if they knew the pilot was alone. ('Lone pilots for cheaper fares' doesn't sound like a great business plan!) The pilot allows the great invention of autopilot to do its job until she is needed to take back control, for example, when turbulence hits, or when landing the plane.

What does this have to do with anxiety?

BEING ANXIOUS DOESN'T ALLOW YOUR AUTOPILOT TO KICK IN.

Your brain has limited resources, so it delegates tasks in order of priority. If you've convinced yourself that you're in danger (such as losing control of your vehicle while driving), you won't give your brain the option of switching to autopilot because you'll be on constant alert.

Losing control of your vehicle becomes your focus, and your brain will prioritise the survival instinct (fight or flight), putting everything else to the back of the queue. A balanced person will be thinking about what's for dinner, and a high-anxiety sufferer will be concentrating on not crashing the car. What should be a straightforward and everyday task becomes a potential disaster thanks to the 'what if...' scenarios created by your brain.

'What if I have an accident?'

'What if I get trapped on the motorway?'

'What if I never see my family again?'

Can you imagine how a pilot would feel if he thought about the stress and pressure of landing throughout the *entire* journey? It's impossible to live a happy and free life if we're in a constant state of alertness. That's partly why learning to reduce stress by using your autopilot is crucial. It gives your brain the essential rest periods it needs – and deserves.

The ironic thing about our autopilot is, the more you think about it, the less likely it is to kick in. It's a natural process, and your brain needs to feel confident enough to let it happen, which means being less anxious and on edge. It might feel a little strange at first, especially if it hasn't happened for a while, but when your autopilot is activated you should be reassured by the fact you're well on your way to revival.

Do you feel safe?

Where do you feel most safe? Home is the usual answer – my 'safe place' was home. If you think about it, your home is nothing more than bricks and mortar plus a few possessions, so what is it that *really* makes you feel safe?

FAMILIARITY

When you're highly anxious, you will naturally seek comfort, and the way to get it is through familiarity. There is a part of the brain called the amygdala, and this is responsible for emotional reaction and the processing of memory. High anxiety doesn't like unknown territory (unfamiliarity) because it perceives it as a potential threat, and it's the amygdala that's in control of this thought process.

I knew my home. I knew what and where everything was. I knew if I felt particularly anxious I could go to my bedroom and put my blanket over my head. I couldn't do that anywhere else and, even if I could, it wouldn't be in an environment I was familiar with, so I'd still feel uncomfortable. The amygdala is responsible for making you feel on edge in unfamiliar territory. It screams out to you, 'Please, go back to what you know!' It's the reason you stay in your 'safe place'. It thinks it's helping to protect you and keeping you away from danger and, although this may be true, the reality is that it's actually having a detrimental effect on your life – especially if you're unable to leave your home.

Before you go to the doctor and ask to have your amygdala removed, it's unfortunately not that straightforward. It's well and truly implanted in the middle of your brain. Because you're stuck with it, there's only one solution – teach it that not everything in life is an immediate threat to your survival. Teach it that going to the supermarket isn't going to kill you, leaving your house doesn't mean you're going to die, and seeing friends doesn't mean impending doom!

The good news is the amygdala can be retrained, with practice and time. You might get so good at retraining it that you're able to go out and do the things you wouldn't have dared to do, even before the days of high anxiety. You might be able to book that bungee jump and skydive you've always wanted to do sooner than you think! OK, let's take it one step at a time...

We're all unique, with a different tolerance to unfamiliarity and thresholds to acceptable anxiety. Anxiety comes in many forms, and it's important you're able to differentiate between normal and high anxiety.

Confusing the two can result in the belief that you're suffering a lot more than you actually are.

High anxiety?

It's normal for everybody to experience anxiety and stress on a daily basis. While writing this book, I was anxious to release it and help as many people as possible. When crossing a busy road, anxiety helped me to make the decision to jog across to avoid the fast-approaching car that was about to squash me!

We should all expect anxiety to be with us every day.

The easiest way to distinguish high anxiety from normal anxiety is to look at your overall life, and how you make decisions. With normal levels of anxiety, going to the supermarket and meeting friends should be straightforward. If at any stage you feel anxious about doing everyday activities like these, and you start to overthink them, high anxiety is taking over. That's when you know you need to stop and think about what's going on, and establish why you're thinking the way you are, so you can do something about it.

If a friend invites you to skydive with them and you decline the invitation because the thought of it makes you panic, that's normal! Skydiving is an extreme sport and it's not for everybody. Everybody is unique and has a different threshold of acceptance. Does it make you a stronger person if you don't decline the invitation? Maybe. We shouldn't hold back from doing the things we want to do because of fear. However, there is always a chance that an extreme sport could go wrong, and if you're not willing to take that chance, that's your choice – that's common sense.

I used to own a motorbike. I loved the speed and the feeling of freedom it gave me. I then had a daughter and, knowing how dangerous motorbikes can be, I decided not to ride one any more. I made what I thought was a smart choice based on the facts I had to hand, and so I sold my bike.

Because we're all different, only you can know if you're being held back by fear or if you're making a sound choice based on facts. It is worth noting that high anxiety has a good way of making you boring. 'Stay in the little box I've created for you and don't come out!' This attitude will lead to three things – being uptight, short-tempered and anal! We need to take risks in life to keep us alive. We need a healthy dose of uncertainty to keep us interested. Sometimes you need to rebel against anxiety and teach it that you're not willing to conform to its boring ways! The way to do that is through the power of thought.

The power of thought

I met a therapist who once likened the recovery process from high anxiety to recovering from a broken leg. I agree, there are similarities, including the healing and recovery process involved in both, but I believe there are two fundamental differences that highlight the power of thought. They are:

1. physicality
2. time.

You can't *think* your way out of a broken leg. It's a broken leg; there isn't much you can do about it. With mental illness, there are no physical elements that restrict revival, apart from those created by you.

'Whether you think you can or you think you can't,
you're right.'
- Henry Ford

What do you think? I believe, with the power of thought, you can literally think your way out of anything, including anxiety and depression. How else are you going to do it? If you don't believe that revival is possible, you're right.

Have you heard of people who have defied all odds and recovered from horrific injuries? People who have been told they'll never walk again, only to do exactly that? People diagnosed with life-threatening diseases, given months to live, and go on to live for many years? What's the difference between these people and the people who never recover, never walk again, and die? To that, unfortunately I don't have the answer. There's a much higher power governing it all. I do, however, have some beliefs, and one of them is in the power of thought.

Your physical body can only do so much – but how much? The world's strongest man competition is full of athletes of a similar stature, and they all spend hours at the gym training and lifting weights. If they're all so similar, what separates the champion from the person who comes second, or third, or tenth? Does being naturally gifted count? Maybe, but what if the champion wasn't as big as the person who came second, or couldn't train as hard as the person who came third, because of an injury? They're all exceptionally strong human beings, so what is it that sets the champion apart? I believe the power of thought plays an important part. The champion wouldn't be the champion if he didn't *believe* he was going to win, even before the competition started.

How does the power of thought and belief relate to overcoming anxiety and depression?

You have to *believe* you can overcome anxiety and depression, otherwise you'll never win the competition.

You're not going to think your way out of a broken leg. It requires a resting period to allow nature to take its course. However, the power of thought is still part of the healing process, because nature is aided by strong mental wellbeing.

The major difference between a broken leg and overcoming anxiety and depression is there are no physical limitations or time restraints. You dictate how quick or slow you want your revival to be.

High anxiety is a habit, so you will naturally go through a healing and recovery process, just like with a broken leg. You will need time and practice because you have to adjust to your new balanced life but, again, it's up to you how quickly you want to do it.

Forgetting to be anxious

I mentioned earlier in the book that everybody has to have a turning point in order for change to happen. My turning point – the thing that changed everything for me – was at the supermarket, which, as I mentioned earlier, was a particular challenge for me. The bright lights beaming down, the crowds of people pushing past me, and the feeling that the floor was swallowing me up always made for an unpleasant experience.

I generally avoided supermarkets like the plague, but I decided to brave it because I wanted to cook my partner a special meal for her birthday. I put my brave face on, and in a hurry headed out to the local supermarket. As I walked through the entrance the usual wobbly legs and dizziness hit me, but I was determined and continued walking, concentrating on my shopping list. I darted around the aisles looking for the ingredients, and had been shopping for about five minutes when all of a sudden I thought, 'Why am I not feeling anxious?' I actually stood still in the aisle, wondering why I hadn't had a panic attack. Previous visits to the supermarket had always resulted in panic in one form or another, and I couldn't believe it hadn't hit me yet.

I was so engrossed by the ingredients I needed to buy, I forgot to be anxious!

As soon as I reminded myself that I was in a supermarket, I started to have the symptoms of a panic attack. In an instant I started to feel dizzy, disorientated and overwhelmed by fear. Normally, that would be enough for me to drop my basket and run towards the nearest exit, but this time it was different, very different.

With all the symptoms of panic rushing through my body, I remember standing in the middle of the supermarket in a state of calm. Thoughts of 'get the hell out of here' and 'you need to leave now' raced through my mind, but I told them to be quiet. At that moment everything fell into place.

Because I had to remind myself to be anxious, it meant that I was creating those feelings, so I was in *total* control.

This revelation put everything into perspective. It exposed anxiety for what it really was. This complicated condition that had haunted me for fifteen long years all became so simple.

I DIDN'T RUN AWAY FROM THE FEAR.

As I stood in the supermarket, feelings of panic continued to try to consume me, but for the first time I felt in absolute control. I still felt dizzy and disorientated, but with one fundamental difference – I didn't care. I knew I had created those feelings, and therefore I had nothing to fear. I didn't run away from the fear, and saw it for exactly what it was – a physical feeling I had created.

By forgetting to be anxious, it indisputably confirmed that high anxiety was a habit – a behaviour conditioned over a period of time.

With a slight smile, I walked calmly to the checkout. I still felt a little dizzy, but that was OK. I didn't expect my symptoms to disappear immediately. I was happier with the fact that my feelings were subsiding rather than accelerating. I was more proud of the fact that I'd stood my ground and not run to the exit. I paid for my shopping and walked to my car. As I packed my shopping in the boot, I felt a profound sense of calm I hadn't felt for a long time.

This was my turning point – and the biggest step I made towards my revival.

What are you *really* afraid of?

When I refer to anxiety, I'm referring to *all* anxiety-related disorders. That's because they're all connected to the same four-letter word – FEAR.

Everything is linked to fear.

Stress = Fear = Anxiety
Worry = Fear = Anxiety
Disorders = Fear = Anxiety
Phobias = Fear = Anxiety
Panic attacks = Fear = Anxiety
Depression = Fear = Anxiety

If you want to get technical, you could place fear anywhere in these equations. It will just as happily go before stress, or after anxiety. That's because fear is part of everything we do, including why, when and where we do it. Whether you decide to stay at home, go to work, see friends or stay in bed, fear informs your decision.

We all experience different levels of fear, and the strongest fear(s) you believe in will always dictate what you do. For example, if you're more scared of your boss than you are about the consequences of not working, it's likely you won't go to work. I appreciate it isn't nice to think you're doing everything based on fear, and you're not. You also do things because they create positive emotions, including being happy (working earns you money, and money can buy you things that make you happy).

But whether or not you like it (or even want to think of it in this way), fear will always be part of your decisions. We live by a set of 'have tos'. These are similar to our 'wants', but they live deeper in our subconscious. They shape you as a person, and govern your actions. 'Have tos' are formed by a number of factors, including the expectations we put on ourselves, and the expectations of others. They are always driven by your greatest fears. We will cover 'have tos' in more detail in Part 3.

'Too many of us are not living our dreams because we are living our fears.'
- Les Brown

Put simply, fear is a feeling that *you* create, generated from a thought or belief.

So, if we agree that we create fear, doesn't that mean we have a choice? Doesn't that mean if you change some of the beliefs you possess – beliefs that might have been holding you back for some time – you can change how you feel? Doesn't it mean that the feeling of fear is as weak or as strong as you make it? Before I expand on this further, it helps to understand fear a little better, including why phobias exist.

Most people with a phobia generally have a misconception about what it is they really fear. For example, you might think it's the snake (object) you're scared of, but you're actually afraid of being bitten (the cause), and what would happen to you if you were bitten (possible death).

How does this relate to being anxious?

It's not anxiety you fear – it's the *cause* of anxiety:

- Having a panic attack and dying.
- Going insane and losing your mind.
- Losing everything you have.

This is a great bit of knowledge to have, because it will help you to rationalise and understand what it is you *really* fear. It should also help to take away the 'unknown' and hand back control to you.

So, let's get to the *real* cause of your fears.

Getting to the *real* cause

High anxiety caused me a lot of confusion and frustration. I couldn't understand why I felt anxious in situations that didn't call for it. I could be sitting at home watching TV when – *BOOM!* – a feeling of complete panic and detachment would come from nowhere. Hot flushes, dizziness, sweating and all the other delightful symptoms would just hit me. I wasn't in any danger – a lion wasn't sitting watching TV with me – so what was the cause?

This is extremely common, so you can probably relate to this. Anxiety has most probably crept up on you when you least expected it to. The good news is I have a solution for this, and it's all about *exposing your fear*. By giving anxiety a new meaning (fear), it puts it into perspective, so rather than asking yourself why you feel anxious, the real question should be: *'What am I afraid of?'*

What am I afraid of?

I mentioned earlier that I'm a big advocate of talking therapies, including counselling. A good counsellor will help you get to the root cause of your fears, and that's important. You have to understand what you *really* fear before you can deal with it. Some fears are a little more complicated than others, and might need professional help to dig them out. If you think that might be you, go and find an experienced therapist straightaway.

While you set out on your fear-finding mission, I came up with a simple technique that helped me break down my fears and get to the root cause of them. It's something I still use today on a daily basis, because it works so well.

It's asking the question: **WHY?**

Example
Being housebound due to agoraphobia, I described my fear as 'leaving my house'. Let's start with that.

Q: What are you afraid of?
A: Leaving my house.

Q: *Why* are you afraid to leave your house?
A: I can't face the outside world.

Q: *Why* can't you face the outside world?
A: Because it scares me.

Q: *Why* does it scare you?
A: I'm afraid of being trapped.

Q: *Why* are you afraid of being trapped?
A: Because feeling trapped makes me have a panic attack.

Q: *Why* are you scared to have a panic attack?
A: A panic attack makes me believe I'm going to die, and I'll be embarrassed if other people see me having one.

By continually asking 'why' I established that leaving my house wasn't the real cause of my fear; it was the possibility of dying from a panic attack and what other people thought of me.

When will I know I've reached the real cause of my fear?

Some people will be better at this than others.

At first, I found it hard to get to the real cause of my fears. I was in complete denial, and I didn't want to face up to them. This is another reason why I needed help from a professional – my denial was keeping me from the truth, and I needed help to face my fears and bring them to the surface. Until you get used to facing up to your challenges and fears, and recognising what they really are, professional help might be required.

You'll know when you get to the real cause of your fear when you're able to deal with it.

False
Evidence
Appearing
Real

It's important to master the skill of breaking a problem down by asking 'why', for two reasons:

1. No matter how big or challenging a problem is, when you break it down and establish its real cause, it makes it easier and much more straightforward to manage. You get rid of the unknown and prevent any further fear.
2. The perceived enormity of a problem will make you believe that you can't cope with it, causing more anxiety. When you break it down you'll realise that it's not that big, and you *can* deal with it.

Being afraid to leave my house was too big a problem for me to deal with. Because I thought that was my fear, I couldn't deal with it. When I reinforced this belief with the possibility of failure, I gave up and accepted it. I coped with it as well as possible, which meant me being agoraphobic for over three months. When I broke down the fear, I discovered that its root cause was having a panic attack and dying. When I knew that's what I was dealing with, I could do something about it.

Try this – it might help:

Spend five minutes thinking about your disorders and phobias (fears).

Break them down and find their real cause by continually asking *why*? It might help if you wrote them down.

If you completed the above task correctly, you'll find the real cause of your fear always comes back to one or both of these things:

- Death
- People.

I call it the *DP rule.*

The DP rule

Death

A morbid subject, I know, but one we have to cover. Death seems very extreme, but if you're honest, this is ultimately what you fear. It is, of course, irrational, but most fears are, and high anxiety isn't known for its reason. The fear of death goes back to how we abuse the fight or flight system, and perceive something to be a threat to our survival. You can link the fear of death to all anxiety-related disorders.

Panic attacks
Symptoms such as heart palpitations and chest pain cause you to think you might have a heart attack and die.

Health anxiety (hypochondria)
Constantly checking your body for changes, and thinking you might have a serious illness that will kill you: for example, a headache isn't just a headache, it's a life-threatening brain tumour.

Obsessive compulsive disorder (OCD)
If you don't complete a ritual there will be a consequence, which might result in your death, or the death of somebody close to you.

Post-traumatic stress disorder (PTSD)
If you've witnessed a traumatic event or somebody close to you has died, it increases your belief that the same could also happen to you.

Phobias

Common phobias include the fear of flying (a plane crash), insects (being bitten) and heights (falling from a height). All result in death.

'Death is not the greatest loss in life.
The greatest loss is what dies inside us while we live.'
- Norman Cousins

As an anxiety sufferer, I liked to stay firmly in control, which meant knowing things. None of us really knows what death is, making it one of the big unknowns. That's why I feared it as much as I did – I couldn't control it and didn't have a clue what it was, what it meant, and what happens when you die. Today, I'm less scared of death, mainly because I've accepted its inevitability. When I put my rational head on, I don't see the point in fighting or worrying about something that is unavoidable. Like so many other worries, it will eat you up inside if you let it, causing never-ending anxiety.

What has worrying ever done for you anyway, including worrying about death? It's not going to stop you dying, is it? I know worrying has never had a positive effect on my life. Wouldn't you rather spend your time living your life and focusing on what really matters? The only thing that really matters is you living your life how you want to live it, without fears and worry bringing you down. A lot of time, energy and emotion can go into fearing death. It can paralyse you into submission. Learning to accept its inevitability is crucial to overcome its potential power over you. Stop wasting your time, and start living.

PEOPLE

Do you know what our number-one fear is?

Death? No – that normally comes about fourth on the list.

Spiders? No – they also come a little further down the list.

The consistent number-one fear we have is *public speaking*. If you think about it, it's just another way of saying that our number-one fear is other people. Imagine you're the only person on the planet. Would you suffer from:

- Social anxiety?
- Separation anxiety?
- Performance anxiety (stage fright)?

No, because all of these anxieties (fears) are associated with other people, otherwise they wouldn't exist. So, why do we fear people, and why are we so concerned about what other people think of us?

APPROVAL

As human beings, we have fundamental needs. The need for approval has been implanted in us from the moment we were born, which is why, in one way or another, we seek approval from everybody we meet. Not convinced? Try going to the supermarket in just your underwear! As humans, we also seek reassurance if we are feeling apprehensive and uncertain, thanks to fear. By asking 'is this OK?', the responsibility doesn't rest solely on you, and by getting reassurance from others you counteract the feeling of uncertainty created by fear. In other words, a problem shared is a problem halved. That's why separation anxiety can spiral out of control when the person you've come to depend on for reassurance is not there any more. If you've let the gap between your own self-belief and the reassurance from others get too big, it can be hard to fill.

It starts young

I grew up in a single parent family, which meant we had to be thriftier than the average. I remember going to school wearing a pair of training shoes that weren't one of the well-known, 'cool' brands. I was laughed at and made to feel like a complete outsider. I went home that day concocting a plan for how I could damage them so badly that I'd never have to wear them again. I decided that I'd accidentally lose them, which completely backfired on me. My mum couldn't afford to buy any others, so I ended up having to wear plimsolls! If you're not familiar with plimsolls, they are the laughing-stock of all the shoe varieties. The kids at school the next day certainly reminded me of that fact.

I also remember the kid who had the latest branded trainers. They cost £125 (which was a small fortune in the 1980s) and you could pump them up using the tongue, which was the latest craze. Other kids would flock around him just to have a go of his pump. Those trainers made him the coolest kid in school.

Wearing designer clothes, driving a flashy sports car, and living in a big house are just a few examples of things we do to fit in. Nowadays, keeping up with the Joneses seems to be more important than happiness. Why? We absolutely crave approval, which sometimes means we forget about what's really important in life, like being happy.

Fear is created by other people's expectations, and stress is produced by the thought of not gaining their approval.

This is why the workplace is the cause of so much anxiety. The job itself might be demanding, but it's the pressure we put on ourselves and the pressure from others that creates the anxiety. Tyrant bosses are one of the biggest causes of excessive stress and anxiety, especially when they have the people skills of a gnat.

I work for myself and don't have a boss, so this doesn't apply to me, does it?

The same principle applies to anybody you answer to, including your clients. Stress and anxiety will come from any form of expectation, so the cause in this case is your need to satisfy your clients and maintain good customer service levels, otherwise you'll go out of business. If you own a business with shareholders, the shareholders will expect to get a return on their investment, and this could trigger feelings of anxiety.

In all of these circumstances, the underlying fear is the expectations you put on yourself. Some are realistic, and others aren't. For example, the need to earn money is realistic, because if you don't, who is going to pay the bills and put food on the table? However, it's unrealistic to think you can work fourteen hours every day to achieve it and stay balanced – especially if you're just trying to keep up with the Joneses.

Learning to love yourself (and others)

Whenever I felt anxious and depressed, I was always quick to criticise others. Picking fault and finding reasons for not liking people was easy. I became very bitter towards others, and blamed them for feeling as awful as I did. I was looking at it completely wrongly. The reality was, I was feeling sorry for myself. In my highly anxious state of mind it was easier for me to blame others. It was easier for me to stay at home blaming everybody else for the way I felt. It was only when I understood that I was in complete control of how others made me feel that I started to embrace them. Knowing I held this power meant I could develop friendships and relationships based on trust, without a hidden agenda.

'Do not let the behaviour of others destroy your inner peace.'
- Dalai Lama

You're only going to find peace within yourself when you don't allow anybody else to dictate or control your emotions.

It was up to me how somebody else's words made me feel. I could choose to take what they said with a pinch of salt, or continuously replay their words in my mind until they became so emotionally crippling I couldn't take any more, and therefore avoid any further hurt by removing people from my life.

There are currently over seven billion people on the planet. Like it or loathe it, social interaction is a fundamental part of any healthy lifestyle, which makes overcoming social anxiety (and all fears related to other people) a priority. You don't need to become the socialite of the century, but it's important to feel comfortable around others. A good start is to stop continuously picking fault and criticising others, and learning to sympathise by understanding and accepting people for who they are. Hate and bitterness will eat you up inside, and knock your BALANCE completely out of sync. Love, empathy and acceptance will help you grow, and significantly reduce your anxiety.

'Love yourself – accept yourself – forgive yourself – and be good to yourself, because without you the rest of us are without a source of many wonderful things.'
- Leo F. Buscaglia

Another big priority, before learning to love others, is learning to look in the mirror and love what you see. You can't do one without the other.

'I don't deserve to be happy.'

'I can't break this anxiety.'

'My life will never change.'

These are just a few of the thoughts I used to beat myself up with every day. I would look in the mirror and really dislike the person looking back. I used to wonder how I'd let my life get so bad, and blame myself for it. Why would anybody want me around them?

All of this was part of me feeling sorry for myself.

If these sound familiar, remember that you owe it to yourself to achieve what you want in life. You *do* deserve to be happy, and you *can* break the pattern. Your life will change if you want it to. You are as special and deserving as anybody else on this planet. Suffering from anxiety and depression doesn't change the fact that you are human and possess the same abilities as anybody else, including me. Never let anxiety and depression make you doubt this.

Love yourself – you have a lot to offer.

Start believing this, and the rest will follow, including overcoming your fear of others.

Like magic

Along with the fear of death and people (the DP rule), depression is a further cause of anxiety-related disorders, which is why they tend to go hand in hand. Death and people are two short-term causes of fear that result in immediate effects (such as a panic attack), whereas depression is a longer-term cause. For example, depression alone isn't going to induce a panic attack, but will work with the fear of death and people as the overall cause of your anxiety.

Take bullying, for example. If you're being bullied, the immediate fear of the person bullying you can cause a panic attack. If the bullying continues it will get you down, and over a period of time it will make you depressed. Being depressed will cause more anxiety, which can result in further anxiety disorders, such as agoraphobia.

BULLYING = PANIC ATTACKS = DEPRESSION = AGORAPHOBIA = MORE ANXIETY AND DEPRESSION

The symptoms of depression were brutal for me. The continuous cycle of anxiety-induced depression made it extremely difficult to get out of bed in the morning – so most days I didn't. Pulling the blankets over my head was the easy option (I thought, at the time), and I took it. When anxiety and depression are working so effectively together, they are tough nuts to crack, but there is a way, and the DP rule will help.

Why is the DP rule a good thing?

Knowing that you can link your fear back to just two things (death and people) is great news. It makes dealing with your fear much more straightforward. Focusing on the DP rule also eliminates insecurities and feelings associated with the unknown, because you know exactly what you have to deal with: the fear of death and/or people – that's it. If I haven't given you enough good news to fill you with confidence and reassurance, I have some more:

DEALING WITH FEAR MAKES SYMPTOMS DISAPPEAR!

At the peak of my high anxiety my symptoms were numerous. I could write out a long list, but let's use the two most prevalent physical symptoms I experienced:

- Chronic indigestion (a constant tight feeling in my chest)
- Neck ache.

The symptoms seemed to be unrelated, but once I had dealt with my fear of death and people, which in turn dealt with my anxiety and depression, over time *all* my symptoms disappeared – like magic. I thought it would take a long time for each symptom to disappear, but they fell like dominos.

The tight dull pain in my chest disappeared.

The tension around my head, which I was once convinced was a brain tumour, disappeared.

Neck ache, muscle tension and cramps disappeared.

The smothering sensation and feelings of breathlessness disappeared.

My mind became clear of unnecessary and irrational fears, and anxiety-related disorders became non-existent.

I was no longer afraid to go outside, and agoraphobia had no hold over me.

I didn't have to follow routines and ritual behaviours caused by obsessive thoughts – I was no longer afraid of the 'consequences'.

I was comfortable in social situations because I didn't seek approval or reassurance.

I challenged a panic attack to start whenever it wanted to, and knew I could deal with it at any time.

I became more positive about the future, and my depressive, cynical state of mind became optimistic.

I no longer worried about the small things.

I could fall asleep with ease, and didn't wake in a cold sweat.

The same will happen to you when you overcome your fear of death and people.

PART 2: TECHNIQUES TO REDUCE ANXIETY AND INCREASE ENERGY

Rational thinking

I'm glad high anxiety isn't a salesperson knocking on my door, because I'd be the reluctant owner of whatever it was selling! It has the most unique way of making you believe all the irrational and bizarre thoughts your brain can muster and, boy, is it good at it! How can we break its hold on us, and be confident enough to tell it to go away, if we don't want to buy what it's selling?

RATIONAL THOUGHT

The first step in dealing with any situation or problem and reducing levels of anxiety is to comprehend it. I say comprehend rather than understand, because this is part of the problem. A person suffering from high anxiety is constantly looking for answers, researching symptoms, and in need of ongoing reassurance. This is all counterproductive. Because you're so keen to control everything you'll try to predict and understand everything that's going to happen, even if that means making up ridiculous concepts. Think about how much of what you think actually happens. If 100% of your predictions for the future have come true, please get in touch – you and I can make some serious money!

Your time and energy is better spent acting on a solution, rather than spending hours trying to understand it. If your car breaks down you wouldn't need weeks, months or years of training before you fix it – you'd simply take it to a garage and have a mechanic inspect and fix it. You don't need to thoroughly understand anxiety to overcome it – leave that to the professionals. Unless you decide you want to become an expert on a subject, comprehension is all you need.

Once you achieve an appropriate level of comprehension (which covering Part 1 should have done for you), rationalise. Most fears (anxieties) are based on completely irrational beliefs. Take the fear of flying, for example. There are more than twenty million flights every year, and flying remains one of the safest ways to travel. It's natural for a developed brain to go through a 'should I, shouldn't I?' stage when making a decision, and even the most seasoned travellers go through the same thought process. After considering all the factors, including their survival, they continue to fly. Why?

They use rational thinking.

We all play with odds in life. The chances of a plane crashing are extremely low, and although our natural thought process factors in dangers and threats, most people will happily board a plane because the chance of a disaster actually happening is so low. They concentrate on the end goal, which might be lying on a beach somewhere, rather than focusing on the minuscule chance that the plane might crash.

By putting a stop to the habitual irrational beliefs created by the anxious brain, you will put things into perspective, allowing you to turn negative beliefs into positive outcomes. You'll focus on the end goal, and that will become your true destination. You don't have to look at worst-case scenarios when thinking rationally. The reality is, things rarely ever get close to being that bad – especially after you've done them. Don't let anxiety and depression convince you otherwise. I've seen individuals who have been able to overcome their fears using rational thinking alone.

Key steps that will help you deal with an anxious thought include the following:

Anxious thought

↓

Continually ask 'Why?' to establish the real cause of your fear

↓

Link the fear back to the DP rule

↓

Use rational thinking to overcome the fear

Panic attacks

You may be surprised to read that I'm not going to cover panic attacks in great detail. Why? Because I know how quickly they subside once you start to get your BALANCE in order. They are just another one of the symptoms that will disappear.

Rather than giving you dozens of pointless techniques on how to stop them, your focus is better spent on getting your BALANCE right – which is your number-one priority. Everything else will follow, including saying goodbye to panic attacks for good. What is important, however, is being educated on what a panic attack is, and that's what we will concentrate on.

Stop the bully

Panic attacks flourish in vulnerable, highly anxious minds, which is why I like to compare them to a bully. Panic attacks and bullies share many similarities, and let me show you why.

Imagine yourself back at school. Every day in science, Bill has been bullying you. He embarrasses you in front of everybody by calling you spiteful names, and whenever it's time to do an experiment he taunts you by stealing some of your equipment. The bullying gets a little more extreme each time, until it becomes physical, and he takes advantage of the teacher turning to write something on the board by hitting you on the arm. You ask him to stop, beg him, plead with him, even shed a tear, but he takes great pleasure in seeing your anguish and pain, and carries on. Bill makes it clear he'll 'get you' after school if you tell tales, so you don't tell anybody about the bullying and stay quiet because you're afraid of the consequences. Because there are no consequences to his actions, it fuels his behaviour further, and the bullying continues to get worse. It's all you can think of all day, from the moment you get up in the morning to when you lie awake at night. The thought of going into the science class sends shivers down your spine. Bill terrifies you.

Now I'd like to ask you some questions:

1. Do you believe Bill would get as much satisfaction from bullying you if he knew it had no effect on you whatsoever?

YES or NO

2. Would it shock and surprise Bill if, when he hit you on the arm, you reacted by shouting at him, 'Do your worst!'?

YES or NO

3. Do you think confronting Bill is any worse than the prospect of facing him after school or living in terror for the rest of your school days?

YES or NO

There are many forms of bullying in all aspects of life, whether at school, work or home. It doesn't matter how big, small, popular, clever or devilishly handsome you might be; it can happen to anybody as long as one key element exists:

YOU ALLOW IT TO HAPPEN.

You decide how much or little power a bully (panic attack) has over you, or whether it exists at all.

A bully's intention is to cause you mental (and sometimes physical) upset because they gain perverse pleasure from seeing you in distress. It makes them feel strong and powerful, which is why pleading, crying and begging with them don't work. Don't waste your time wondering why they're doing what they do – you'll probably never understand their twisted mind, which is a good thing. Why would you want to understand their reasoning? Who cares? Your focus should be on putting a stop to it.

Like a bully, if you don't give a panic attack the reaction it craves, it will stop. **There is no fuel to stoke the fire**. It will get fed up and leave you alone. If you confront a panic attack and hit it back by saying 'Do your worst!', it won't get worse, it will get better. Can you imagine the look on Bill's face if you did that to him? He would be horrified! Initially, his pride will be dented, so to save face it may force him to react, but he'll eventually get fed up and stop. If there's no fuel stoking his fire it will burn out.

Keep putting the fire out – you are the smarter, bigger person.

The emotions generated by determination and tenacity (with a sprinkling of anger) are greater than those of a panic attack. Try it. Next time you feel like you might have a panic attack, hit it back and shout, 'DO YOUR WORST!' You don't have to physically shout it out if people are around; shout it internally. Just make sure that, when you say it, you really mean it – show the bully you mean business. It might be scary at first, but nobody said that facing a bully isn't scary. I can, however, give you a guarantee that it is no scarier than the prospect of living a life in fear, tormented by not knowing when the next panic attack may strike.

'Do not judge me by my successes; judge me by how many times I fell down and got back up again.'
- Nelson Mandela

You've allowed panic attacks to control you, probably for some time, so adjustment is needed. If Bill had bullied you every day for the past few years, and all of a sudden you decide that's it not going to happen any more, he needs to get used to the fact he can't do it any more. A bit of time and adjustment is needed.

If I adopt this attitude, how long will it take before panic attacks stop?

The most important thing, from this day forward, is deciding that you won't allow panic attacks to continue to bully you. The psychological significance and power this gives you could mean that you never suffer one again.

Stop punishing yourself

By saying 'stop punishing yourself', are you suggesting that I'm my own bully?

Yes, I am. This doesn't mean that you get pleasure from causing yourself psychological harm, because you don't get any gratification from it. Have you ever met anybody who has enjoyed having a panic attack? Of course not. So, if you don't get pleasure from a panic attack, how does your bully exist?

YOUR BULLY IS BORN FROM HABIT.

Like high anxiety, panic attacks exist thanks to conditioned behaviour. You've taught yourself to react to the fight or flight response with a panic attack, and the symptoms of a panic attack have been bullying you. Over time, the bullying has become more extreme and frequent, because you give it meaning by providing the reaction and fuel it needs to survive.

It's your choice whether or not you have a panic attack, and it's just as easy to decide not to have one. If a panic attack lasts for ten seconds or ten days (or whether it starts at all, for that matter), you dictate that. **You are in absolute control** of how you react to 'feelings', and when you realise that you hold this absolute power, you can stop panic attacks in an instant.

Why would you want to continue suffering from a condition that causes such misery and discomfort, when you have the power to stop it? There is no logic in suffering a panic attack – it serves you no purpose other than to cause you psychological distress. A genuine need for the fight or flight response is rare, and when it is needed for a life or death situation, it's normally instantaneous. You don't have time to think about it. Your survival instinct is incredible, and your mind and body will work in perfect synchronicity if – and when – you need to deal with real danger. You have been given an automatic response you don't need to worry or think about. Panic attacks are useless to you. Remind yourself just how useless they are next time you start to 'feel' a panic attack coming on.

Remember what a panic attack is

Rational thinking and proven facts will tell you that a panic attack has *never* killed anybody. *They do not cause physical harm*. That means you can gain immediate reassurance by eliminating the fear of death (the DP rule). Feelings of panic are exaggerated by uncertainty, so you can also gain confidence and control by remembering what a panic attack is:

NOTHING MORE THAN THOUGHT PROJECTED INTO FEELING.

I can list any symptom you like, but the fact remains, a panic attack always starts with a thought: what you do with that thought is dictated by you. Next time you 'feel' the sensations of a panic attack, just decide that you're not going to have one. Sound too simple to be true? I challenge anybody who says they're unable to stop a panic attack. Everybody owns the control, and if you own the control, it's completely up to you. **It's your decision.**

With time and practice, the right decision becomes easier and quicker to make, and now you're armed with this information, I'm hoping you'll see panic attacks for the bullies they really are, and won't suffer one again.

The process of a panic attack:

Fearful (anxious) thought
↓
Fight or flight response is activated
↓
Panic attack is induced
↓
The most important part in this process:
it's up to *you* what happens next.

I followed an old Japanese proverb – fall seven times, stand up eight. Follow this principle, and the bully will get fed up and stop.

Representation

Let's start with why I call my method of reducing anxiety Representation, rather than following the crowd and calling it Distraction. You might think, 'what's in a name?' and I agree, but when it comes to distraction, it's significant.

Distraction, the name itself, is completely misleading. It implies that you'll always suffer from high levels of anxiety and the best you can do is distract yourself from it. How uninspiring is that? I don't know about you, but I don't see much point in doing something that has no end goal and nothing to aim for. Where's the incentive? I call it Representation because it's exactly that – the use of an object and emotion that *represents* something significant to you. Distraction is naturally part of its method, but it's important not to think of it as a distraction alone. Distraction only lasts for a short period of time, and it's only a matter of time before anxiety bites again. With Representation, you're building positive memories associated with things important to you, which makes it a powerful tool when you need to use it. It gives you the ability to instantly change your emotional and physical state, and quickly overcome feelings of high anxiety.

Everybody has bad days. Life throws all kinds of stuff at everyone on a daily basis. Because of this, stress and anxiety is inevitable, and I use Representation to overcome it. There's something about watching my favourite inspirational video, looking at pictures of my daughter, or putting on my favourite song that can bring all my stress and anxiety back down to where it should be, in an instant. With practice and over time, it will do the same for you. None of this would work, however, without Representation allowing you to connect with one of your most influential emotions – Gratitude.

Gratitude

Gratitude is lethal, and will instantly destroy any negative and depressive thoughts – something high anxiety feeds off. If you're grateful for everything you have, and not fearful about the things you don't have, it's impossible to allow anxiety to permeate your mind.

Why do dock leaves grow near stinging nettles? Nature always wants to provide us with a solution.

GRATITUDE IS NATURE'S SOLUTION TO ANXIETY.

If you feel grateful every day, your outlook on life will completely change.

Does being grateful mean I shouldn't have ambition or want more out of life?

Not at all, no. In fact, we're going to look at why having a goal is important in Part 3. There is, however, a thin line between being grateful for what we have and wanting more in life. Distinguishing between the two is important.

For example, if you're a multi-millionaire and your goal in life is to keep doubling your money each year, but this goal keeps you in a highly anxious state of mind, why are you doing it? Have you sat down and really thought about why you're doing what you're doing? I've used this example specifically because I've met people who have amassed great fortunes, only to keep running themselves into the ground by working harder than ever before. They've made a million, so now they must make two, or three, or ten. They throw happiness out of the window for the sake of achieving a goal. I understand that their fear of losing the money is probably the driving force behind their actions, but it pays to evaluate our goals and check to see what they're really doing for us.

'True happiness is to enjoy the present, without anxious dependence upon the future, not to amuse ourselves with either hopes or fears but to rest satisfied with what we have, which is sufficient.'
- Seneca

Some people have very little money and material objects, yet they're grateful for *something* in their lives. They don't get eaten up inside with resentment and jealousy. They have very little but they still help others, without giving a second thought to what they don't have or should get in return. Are these people closer to knowing what life is really about? I don't know. What I do know is, if a goal is making you unhappy, you should stop striving for it, especially if you don't need to! Strive to achieve goals that make you happy. Help other people, no matter your current situation, and be grateful for what you have.

There is a TEDx talk by Louie Schwartzberg called 'Gratitude' you can find on YouTube that sums up gratitude better than I ever could. You can also find it on my website www.carlvernon.com.

How to use Representation

With such a powerful emotion, you're going to want to access gratitude as much as possible, particularly at times when you're feeling highly anxious. The three most effective ways to do this include a picture/photo, a collection of songs, and a video/film.

A picture/photo

When I see a picture of my daughter I feel instantly grateful. Your picture could be of anyone close to you (child, partner, friend), or of a time or place you associate with happy memories, such as a party or holiday. You should carry this picture around with you at all times. I find the easiest way to do this is to have it on my mobile phone. It's also a good idea to have physical copies of your photos, so you can stick them to places you look at a lot, like your fridge or dashboard of your car. Every time you look at the picture it should make you thankful and grateful for the gift you were given.

Music

Silence isn't good. It allows your mind to drift off into places you may not want to go. Music is the best remedy for this, and the reason why over 80% of people use it to change their mood. It can fire up emotions, self-belief, positive memories and joy, making it very effective for dealing with anxious thoughts. Again, a mobile phone is the easiest method of carrying your music with you at all times. During the rebalancing period, take your headphones with you wherever you go, and when you feel anxious you can put your headphones in and listen to songs that make you feel happy and grateful.

My taste in music is diverse, and I always have at least five songs I really like at any one time. When I listen to music that makes me happy, I associate it with everything in life I'm grateful for, including my loved ones, my health, and the opportunities I'm continually given to change my life.

Pick the songs that make you feel happy and grateful, create a playlist and call it 'Grateful'. As you listen to the songs more and more, it's natural for the feelings connected to them to become less significant, so keep it fresh by continually changing and adding new songs.

Video | YouTube

One of the best times of my life was when I went to Las Vegas and saw the Blue Man Group. It was an incredible experience, and still puts a smile on my face every time I think about it. I'm very grateful to have been given the opportunity to go and see them, and whenever I watch their videos online it takes me back to all the sensations I felt when I saw them live on stage.

What videos do you watch that allow you to instantly change your state of mind? Like pictures and songs, you can access and watch videos online via a mobile phone, making it the most convenient and immediately accessible tool to carry.

Pick the pictures, songs and videos that make you feel most grateful, and start using Representation today.

Fake it 'til you make it

Our body speaks volumes, and 90% of what we say doesn't come out of our mouth. That means we should give significant appreciation to our physical state.

If I asked ten people to draw somebody who was depressed, they would create a very similar picture. The person would have their head bent, their eyes fixed on the ground, slumped shoulders and an overall look of sadness. It's all part of the package, and taking this physical stance is reinforcing the person's depressive state.

'You must be the person you have never had the courage to be. Gradually, you will discover that you are that person, but until you can see this clearly, you must pretend and invent.'
- Paulo Coelho

In other words: 'fake it 'til you make it!'

And that's exactly my advice for achieving BALANCE. If you're feeling depressed and anxious, your natural reaction is to convey the same thing through your body language. Your brain will be telling your body to show the world how sad and unhappy you are, and how you really feel inside. This negative body language is fuelling your negative emotions, so you have to fight your natural reaction to change your emotion from negative to positive. It's the hardest acting job you'll find in Hollywood because you'll be fighting every instinct in you, but if you really do want to change how you feel, you have to start acting.

Try counteracting negative thoughts and instincts by doing these two things:

1. Smiling
2. Holding your head high.

Smiling tricks your brain into making you think you're happy, even if you're not. Try it. Put a Cheshire cat grin on your face, right now. You might feel instantly better. You might feel ridiculous. Neither matters.

'Peace begins with a smile.'
- Mother Teresa

It will feel unnatural at first, but just keep practising. Fighting against your natural reaction takes intense practice – but it's worth it. It doesn't matter if you don't *feel* like smiling; do it anyway. Remember: fake it 'til you make it! If you think about it, that's all any of us do to achieve what we want – it's just that some of us are better at it than others.

Pride is also a sin you can use to your advantage. Thanks to the DP rule, you're likely to care about what other people think of you more than the average person, so we can use this to improve your body language. Hold your head high. Again, it doesn't matter if you don't *feel* like this is a true reflection of you and your emotions – that's the point!

Changing your persona will change how you feel. Keep smiling, and with time and practice, positivity, happiness, gratitude and optimism will all become reality.

Letting go

When your life is ruled by anxiety and depression it becomes a fairground ride, full of apprehension, mainly caused by your 'what if...?' thoughts. You grab on to life so hard you get white knuckles, and rather than approach a situation in a state of relaxation, your body naturally prepares itself for the worst. Like Bruce Lee preparing to fight, you clench your fists, tighten your muscles (consciously and subconsciously), and grit your teeth, which all amounts to a pretty rough ride.

You need to learn to let go, and appreciate that it's OK not to have complete control.

Tension is at the heart of all your problems, and learning techniques for how to reduce it is key to a balanced life. Tension might manifest itself as a headache, a lump in the throat, or a tight feeling in the chest, but most symptoms can be traced back to tension.

'Take rest; a field that has rested gives a bountiful crop.'
- Ovid

When I concentrated on my body I was surprised by how tense I was. I noticed how much I frowned. How high my shoulders were lifted. How rigid my head and neck were. How curled-up my toes were, and how tightly my fists were clenched. Subconsciously, I was tensing my muscles to counteract the feelings of anxiousness, which only resulted in me being tenser. Although I didn't think about it at the time, I also used tension consciously – I would tense the muscles in my chest to try and regain control from the constant dull pain. Trying to resolve tension with tension was counterproductive, because ultimately I was still tense.

If you're not sure how tense you are, next time you're watching television (or any other activity that activates your autopilot), become consciously aware of your muscles in areas that are typically affected by tension, including:

1. Dropping your shoulders.

2. Releasing tensed and scrunched facial muscles.

3. Loosening your tight grip.

When you become aware of how tense you are, you might feel it across your entire body. Wherever and however you feel it, it should help you to appreciate the constant strain it's putting on your body (both physically and mentally).

You have to learn to let go and relax!

Tension plays a big part in the fear cycle, and using relaxation techniques to release you from the constant feeling of stress and alertness will considerably reduce your levels of anxiety.

Relaxation techniques

Below I've listed some popular relaxation techniques. Over the years I have tried them all and have stuck with the ones that worked for me. I advise you to do the same. There are lots of books and more information available on any technique that appeals to you.

Most importantly, find time to do them as often as possible, especially while trying to re-establish your BALANCE. There is no point working hectically from Monday to Friday and trying to relax at weekends – it won't work. The stress and tension created in the week will carry into the weekend. Relax each evening before you go to sleep. It gives each day closure, helps you sleep, and gets you ready for the next day.

Deep breathing
When you practise deep breathing, you breathe in slowly and deeply, while expanding your belly, allowing your diaphragm to contract. Breathing in this way sends a message to your brain to calm down and relax, which also makes it effective for dealing with panic attacks. It is a simple and versatile technique that can be learned and used immediately.

Progressive muscle relaxation
Progressive muscle relaxation is a very effective technique for releasing tension in your muscles: you tense a muscle for a few seconds and then relax it. For example, try clenching your fist for a few seconds and then letting go, releasing the tension so your hand is as loose as possible. Your hand should feel relaxed after doing this a few times. You can use this technique on any muscle in your body, so if you have a particular tense area, you can concentrate on that. The typical areas that affected me included the neck, chest, head (face) and shoulders. If you do this daily, you will condition your muscles to relax much more freely and naturally.

Physical exercise
You need an outlet for your tension so it's not trapped inside and used to create more stress and negative energy. Physical activities are an effective way to release tension, due to the fact you burn energy and feel like you've accomplished something. Yoga and tai chi are known to improve breathing and relaxation, and are therefore good for stress and tension. If you're more of a football or boxing fan, join your local club. The aim is to find a physical activity you enjoy.

Mental exercise
You can channel the release of tension through healthy mental exertion. I can, however, think of a few board games that increase tension rather than reduce it, so if it becomes counterproductive, avoid it! Sitting down to do a crossword is relaxing for some people, and stressful for others. Use your common sense, and if it's not helping you reduce your anxiety and stress, try something else. I always have at least two games of chess

on the go at any one time (on my mobile phone). It's a game I find challenging, but relaxing at the same time.

Meditation

I make sure I take time to find a moment to relax every day, especially if I'm busy and find myself dealing with extra stress. I watched a TEDx talk called 'Consciousness – the final frontier' by Dada Gunamuktananda (try pronouncing that one!), which you can find on YouTube or on my website, www.carlvernon.com. About 14 minutes 20 seconds in, he asks the audience to close their eyes and connect with the outside world. I gave it a go and found it very calming, so I now use it whenever I need to take five and reconnect with my 'self'.

Meditation (or taking a quiet break by closing my eyes and shutting off for a while) also allows me to open my mind and make an effort to be more grateful. I'm probably going to get lots of experienced meditators complaining to me, because the point of meditation is allowing yourself not to think at all, so let me explain before you email me! Anxiety makes you focus on yourself rather than on the things around you, including the beauty of life. When the mind is under attack from constant racing thoughts, it's difficult to take time to be grateful, and meditation (taking a quiet break) will allow you the time and space to do exactly that.

Have a clear-out

There is no better remedy than having a good clear-out. The more possessions we have, the more emotional attachment we have. This emotional attachment isn't always negative, and you'll likely have possessions that bring you great joy. At the end of your clear-out, I don't expect you to have an empty home! However, there will be a high percentage of your possessions you just don't need (or want) any more. A good clear-out can make you feel great and can make you feel lighter and clearer. I do it regularly. When I looked at my wardrobe I noticed I tended to wear the same selection of clothing all the time, so all the clothes I hadn't worn for a year, I packed and sent to a charity shop. eBay is marvellous for raising some extra funds from unwanted stuff. You might be surprised by how much you can raise. Maybe the money you raise could go towards a trip, or course?

The TEDx talk 'A rich life with less stuff' by The Minimalists (www.theminimalists.com/tedx) explains this well.

Change of scenery

If you're constantly looking at the same four walls, talking to the same people, or doing the same monotonous tasks or job, you're not presenting your brain with the variety and challenge it needs and deserves. Predictability is boring, and boredom leads to unwanted feelings, including feeling trapped, causing excessive stress and tension. Spice up your life a little. Take a relaxing break, change your scenery, and do something out of the ordinary. Now is a good time...

Still haven't booked anything yet?

You can't think of anything you want to do?

Come on, there are endless things you can do...

What's your passion? Maybe there's a course local to you?

I'll guarantee there's a beautiful part of your country you haven't seen yet...

When was the last time you went on a spontaneous walk, run or bike ride?

...OK. So, my book is too good to put down. I can appreciate that. If you're not going to do something spontaneous right now, I want you to seriously consider doing it very soon. Anxiety doesn't like spontaneity, so it's an important step in changing your mindset.

Do things that make you happy

An obvious one, but how often do you stop and ask yourself, 'What makes me happy?' I would assume, like most other people, very rarely. Life has a habit of keeping you so busy doing the things that *have* to be done every day that you have no time to do the things you *want* to do. It's an important question I'd like you to get in the habit of asking yourself, daily. Put a note up on your mirror saying:

'What is going to make me happy today?'

Or, if you want to be a little more task-focused:

'What can I do today to get me closer to achieving BALANCE and feeling happy?'

Base everything you do around this question. For example, ask yourself, 'Is eating that third slice of cake going to get me closer to achieving BALANCE? Is pushing myself to go to that class (the one I've always wanted to go to but put off because I'm too self-conscious) going to help me feel happier in the long run?'

If you're not doing enough things that make you happy, you'll spend most of your time in a state of unhappiness – or, worse, have no feelings at all. **Happiness is an anxiety-killer**, and *the* most effective method of releasing tension and achieving BALANCE. Make an effort to get more of it in your life.

Special attention

I've done my best not to come across as though I'm giving you typical 'self-help'. If I've achieved that, great. If I haven't, you're the reason I'm writing this part of the book. Some of my advice might come across a little 'self-helpy' (if that's a word!), but that's just because a lot of what you have to do is obvious. I've been where you are now, and I can tell you honestly that doing the things I've suggested will change your life. At the risk of sounding too 'self-helpy' again, it's up to you whether or not you choose to dismiss them, or decide to give them a go. Nobody can force you, and it's completely up to you. I will, however, repeat, that deciding to do these things and taking action will make all the difference.

PART 3:
REALIGN YOUR FOCUS

Your focus is your future

At the height of my high anxiety in 2007 I decided to have lunch in a coffee shop on the high street near where I lived and, although I wasn't a big coffee drinker, I thought I'd fit in with the crowd and have a cup. About halfway through the cappuccino I suddenly felt as if I'd been pumped full of electric charge. I could actually feel the adrenaline coursing through my body. My heart started to pound, I felt light-headed, disorientated, and panicky thoughts raced through my mind. Being a master at covering up my despair, I was able to continue sitting in the coffee shop while all this internal torture was going on, without giving away my feelings. All these symptoms were doing their best to make me jump out of my seat and head straight for the exit, but I stayed rooted to my seat, watching the person on the table across from me. I thought to myself, how is he able to gulp his double espresso and sit calmly reading his newspaper, while I'm ready to climb the walls after half a cappuccino? I spent a long time trying to figure out the answer to this question. A lot of things came to mind.

- Was it the fact he drank a lot of strong coffee?
- Did he have a high caffeine tolerance level?
- Was he able to control the energy rush caffeine produced and shrug it off as normal?

Maybe the answer to all three of these questions is yes, but whatever question is asked, they all link back to the same thing:

FOCUS

In my state of high anxiety, my focus was on being anxious, so caffeine, which is a stimulant, fuelled that focus further and heightened my anxious state. The person who enjoyed the double espresso was focused on reading the newspaper and preparing himself for whatever he was doing that day. Both of our bodies went through the same reaction caused by caffeine, but we responded completely differently because of our focus. That's why some people can enjoy a cup of coffee and use it to relax, while others climb the walls, sometimes at just the thought of having a cup. Again, this is a result of their focus and state of mind.

THE RESULT OF AN ACTION DEPENDS ON YOUR INTENTION.

If you start your journey with anxiety as your focus, it will be there waiting for you with a wry smile on its face, waving at you from the finish line, ready to take you in its arms. If you want to break this pattern and finish a journey (or task, or food, or anything) without feeling anxious, your focus has to be on something else.

When life no longer revolves around anxiety, your focus and state of mind are different.

It's easy to allow anxiety to become your sole focus and, if it is, something as innocent as eating a chocolate bar will be a big decision. 'That chocolate bar is going to give me a sugar boost and cause me anxiety. I'll avoid it.' You have made anxiety your focus and decided on the outcome – before you'd even eaten it – so guess what's waiting for you when you put the wrapper in the bin? I'm not a big chocolate-eater so this decision is not something I face often, but if I do decide to eat chocolate, I accept the fact that my body will get an energy boost due to the amount of sugar it has in it. Chocolate also contains caffeine, and because caffeine is a stimulant, I'll get a boost from that too. Rather than use this energy to panic, I'll use it for something else. I could just as easily decide not to eat chocolate.

I try to avoid caffeine wherever possible. Not because of anxiety, but because it gives me a headache. A headache is my body's way of telling me that a food doesn't agree with me. This presents me with a few options: I can either try to figure out why caffeine gives me a headache and see if I can do something about it, or I can avoid caffeine wherever possible and go for decaf options. I choose the latter because most products have a decaf option, and I don't miss caffeine.

If you had a nut allergy, and eating nuts put your life in danger, you'd avoid eating nuts. You don't have any control over your allergy, so you'll avoid nuts. If you're not eating nuts – or chocolate, or drinking coffee – because of anxiety, then that's a different issue. Millions of people enjoy these products on a daily basis without them causing anxiety, so as long as you have control and no allergy or intolerance, you should also be able to enjoy them. We all go through the same bodily reactions, and there's only one difference between you and the other millions of people – FOCUS.

Whatever decisions you make, whether they're about the food you eat, the concert you want to go to, the restaurant you want to eat at, or the supermarket you want to shop at, it helps if anxiety isn't your focus.

The law of attraction

You may be familiar with the law of attraction, or the book *The Secret* by Rhonda Byrne. If not, the principle behind the law of attraction is basically 'whatever you focus on, you get more of'. I read *The Secret* many years ago at the peak of my high anxiety and depression. I thought it might contain some 'secrets' that could help me. It did, but not in the way I anticipated. It was a very simple little book, and I found it enlightening because of its message – that through the law of attraction you can get more of the things you actually want in life. It's easy to forget such an important notion, but when you think about it, it's glaringly obvious! Focus on anxiety, and guess what? You get more anxiety!

So, it got me thinking…

What if you could use this law of attraction to attract something you actually want in your life? Well, I'm pleased to tell you, you can! Whatever you choose to focus your time and energy on from this moment forward, you're going to get more of it – that's a fact. This isn't some form of witchcraft; it's a power we all possess, and it's our choice how much or little we decide to use it. As with any power, it has to be balanced with other things. The law of attraction is balanced with chance, luck, reason and belief. If it weren't, everybody would win the lottery, right?

The law of attraction is also important because we're all emotionally connected to each other. That's why it's imperative to surround yourself with people who have a positive influence on you and your life. It was only when I had the strength to stop allowing negative people in my life that I appreciated what an adverse influence they had on it. Some of my friends never had a good word to say about anybody, including me. Since I decided to keep them at a distance, I've felt much better for it. I admit, I needed help with this at first. I felt guilty for cutting people out of my life, even though they weren't any good for me. However, the guilt soon faded because (a) I had nothing to really feel guilty about, and (b) I felt much better for it.

Try to avoid negative and cynical individuals who never have anything good to say, otherwise you'll attract more of it yourself. You'll inevitably meet them, but try not to get sucked in. You have to be strong and sometimes a little ruthless. If you keep letting them in your life you *will* attract more negativity. I'm not saying cut everybody out of your life – far from it. Even the most happy-go-lucky individuals will have flaws and bad days. You know the individuals I'm talking about, though – the storytellers who have an excuse for everything. The emotional vampires! Keep them at arm's length, especially while finding your BALANCE. You need as much positivity as you can get. Go looking for it, attract it, and you'll get as much as you want.

Have purpose

I met an anxiety sufferer called Geoff, a gentleman in his sixties. He'd just been made redundant after working for thirty years with the same company. His job was his life, and when he didn't have to get up on Monday morning to start work he felt completely lost. He had worked hard for most of his life only to believe that he no longer had any purpose (which was of course completely untrue) when he retired. He didn't know what to do with his time, and because of that, anxiety became his sole focus until it consumed his life.

WITHOUT A CLEAR FOCUS, ANXIETY WILL HIT YOU HARD BY FEEDING OFF YOUR LACK OF DIRECTION.

A healthy and active lifestyle involves change, and you have to adapt to change by realigning your focus. Whether you've recently retired, been made redundant, your children have grown up, a relationship has ended, or any other significant life event has occurred, be prepared to move with it and concentrate on your future.

Whatever your situation, you will always be needed as long as you put yourself in that position. There will always be somebody who needs your help and will draw strength from you. You are unique and special, and there will be things that you know and have learned that you can pass on to others. You will *always* have a purpose – as long as you make it that way.

Look in the direction you want to go

Learning to ride a motorbike had been an ambition of mine for some time, and after plucking up the courage I decided to go and have lessons. (Extra courage was needed because I was suffering from high anxiety at the time, and still at the stage of not telling a soul about it.) After a few lessons within the teaching complex it was time to go out on the open road! Before I could throw in my 'what if...?' concerns, we were heading out.

Riding on the open road was a little daunting at first. The bike was difficult to control and it took a bit of getting used to, especially changing gear. As we approached a steep bend in the road the instructor started to speak in my earpiece and said: 'As you go around this bend, rather than concentrate on trying to control the bike, look up at where you want to go.' As soon as I put my head up and focused on the end point of the road, the bike naturally moved in that direction. Although I was in control of the bike, it felt like I wasn't doing anything at all. It was as though a natural process had taken over. This was one of the most valuable lessons I learned, because when I started to do the same thing with everything else in my life (focus on the end goal rather than the task itself), things naturally headed in the direction I wanted. Try it for yourself. Look up in the direction you want to go, and then life will take you there.

'It's never too late ... to start heading in the right direction.'
- Seth Godin

It's also important to look in the right direction – and that's forward.

'I used to enjoy going shopping for new clothes.'

'The hustle and bustle never used to bother me.'

'I used to go out every Friday after work and had the time of my life.'

By always looking back at what I 'used to' do, it was incredibly easy for me to believe that things were never going to change. There wasn't anything in the future to look forward to, and the only positives I could draw on were from the past (before the horrible condition took over my life). To break out of this pattern of negative thought and lack of optimism, I had to stop looking over my shoulder and instead face forward. I should only be looking backwards if it allowed me to move forward. I would think: *Is that memory going to give me the motivation to move forward, or is it going to fill me with regret?*

Regret is only good for one thing – fuelling anxiety and depression.

Regret will eat you up if you let it. The only time you should ever look back is if you want to go in that direction, or draw inspiration from what you achieved in the past, which helps you go forward and make change. The present and the future are more important than the past, and it's the decisions you make right now in shaping your future that really count.

If you keep drawing on past negative experiences and live with regret, you'll never move forward.

I'd much rather live a life of 'I tried and learned' (even if I failed, or it didn't go as well as I'd hoped it would) than 'I wish I'd...' – wouldn't you?

Get more 'good' stress

I believe there is such a thing as good stress. I know this because all the years I tried to avoid stress (in every form) I got absolutely nowhere, fast! I was so afraid of what anxiety had in store for me that I didn't bother. I stayed in my comfort zone, which was usually within the four walls of my home. I always looked upon stress as the horrible feeling that caused me great unhappiness and discomfort. Although I was right, I was looking at it in the wrong way. Stress wasn't bad; it was a positive sign that I was moving in the right direction. It was proof that I was pushing the boundaries of my comfort zone, and therefore challenging my anxiety and changing my life.

We all have to do things that we're not comfortable doing: going to the dentist, taking a test, or speaking in front of hundreds of people will cause stress and anxiety. However, rather than seeing stress as a horrible, negative feeling, as something to avoid at all costs, try to see it as positive reinforcement that your life is going in the right direction.

Channel your creativity

High-anxiety sufferers are creative. I don't believe this is a coincidence – you have to be creative to become constantly anxious! There is no doubt in my mind that you have a gift, and allowing this gift to be represented by high anxiety is an injustice.

'Anxiety is the handmaiden of creativity.'
- T.S. Eliot

Instead, channel your creativity into something positive – something that offers a challenge.

Hobbies
The reason I had severe social anxiety is because I didn't have anything to talk about! Nothing was going on in my life. Anxiety kept me locked away in my tiny little world, and no new information entered my mind. That's why having a hobby is important. You learn new things and meet new people, and this gives you something to talk about.

My passion is cooking. It allows me to be very creative. Other creative hobbies could include photography, painting, or learning a new language or instrument. Creative hobbies that include exercise, such as dancing or gardening, are even better.

Use your gift for deep thought and understanding to gain knowledge. Spark your imagination by reading books. Subscribe to magazines on subjects that interest you. Watch documentaries that fascinate you and learn things that will blow your mind – in a positive way. I developed a fascination for astronomy after watching a documentary on the Discovery Channel. Whenever I feel a little anxious or stressed, I often look up at the sky. It helps remind me of my place in the world, and that my problems aren't as big as I think they are.

Volunteer
Voluntary work allows you to help people – without the pressure and stress that can come with paid work. Psychologically, this is very powerful and rewarding. I'm a strong believer in whatever you give out,

you get back. I know most of us have a million and one reasons why we're too busy to do this or that, but if you donate just a little of your time (even if it's just an hour a week) to helping others, you will reap the rewards.

When you decide to leave the highly anxious you behind, you'll appreciate how much time you spent being anxious. This creates a big gap in your life that needs filling. This gap can make it easy to revert to old habits, so keep active and busy, and don't allow yourself time to be anxious. Try several new things until you find something you're passionate about. When you're engaged in something you're really interested in, you'll enjoy yourself so much that you'll 'forget' to be anxious.

Get to know your 'have tos'

I touched on our 'have tos' earlier in the book. To remind you, they are the things that live deep inside you, governing what, where, when and how you do things. They define you as a person, and are the reason why you achieve your ambitions, or decide not to get out of bed. Our 'have tos' are driven by our fears, the expectations we put on ourselves, the expectations of others, and our environment. The way we were brought up also plays a part, but before you blame your parents for your anxiety and depression, your 'have tos' constantly change. What governed them a few years back might not be what's driving them today.

It's important to get to know your 'have tos' (in other words, get to know yourself), because understanding what drives you, motivates you and gets you out of bed each day will make the process of change much easier.

Think of 'have tos' like having a deadline. If you knew you had to complete the revision for your exam by Friday, how much more likely are you to revise than if you had no deadline? The fear of not doing it (the consequences of not passing the exam) will drive you to *have to* do it, otherwise you'll probably fail the exam. If that means something to you, you'll do it. If it doesn't, you won't. I realised some time ago that if I didn't really *have* to do something, I wouldn't. My 'have tos' were weak, and with anxiety and depression hitting me hard, they continued to weaken over time. The things that defined me, that made me who I was, disappeared as quickly as a thought.

'I'm not getting out of bed today.'

'I'm not going to work.'

'I'm not going to that party.'

I'm not undermining the illness that is anxiety and depression. I know first-hand how strong their clutches are, and how hard it is to shake off their grubby hands. But what if your life depended on you getting out of bed, going to work, or going to that party? How quickly would things change then? This is probably true for most of you reading this. You might wake up tomorrow and the last thing you want to do is get out of bed and go to work, but you do it because you are more afraid of losing your house than you are of going to work. Getting up in the morning and going to work are now your 'have tos'. You can either use them to drive you forward and make the changes you want in your life, or use them to create more anxiety. Most of us use them to create more fear and anxiety (I know I did).

If I'm absolutely honest with myself, there was an element of laziness attached to my decisions. Yes, anxiety and depression were doing their best to keep me in the quicksand of despair, but there were days when I knew I was taking the easy option – staying in bed, rather than facing up to my demons. That's why tough love from the people closest to you is sometimes the best type of love. If their expectations don't fall in line with yours (and they shouldn't if you're staying in bed all day), they can be the extra driving force you need for change. If it wasn't for my partner Lisa pushing me at times, there is no doubt in my mind that I wouldn't have revived as quickly as I did. I would have taken longer to come to the decision that things needed to change.

As I mentioned earlier, it's vital to have the right people around you. If you spend all day with somebody who doesn't get out of bed, doesn't work, and doesn't socialise, you probably won't either. If you spend your time with ambitious individuals who are proactive and take action to change their lives, you probably will too. It's not guaranteed – the decision is yours, and you will always be in control of your 'have tos' – but if you have positive people in your life, pushing you and giving you tough love when you need it, revival is much more likely to come sooner.

Have a goal

If you want to feel less anxious, you need to start focusing on the things you do want, and that means having a goal. A goal will keep your eyes on the prize, which is important, because when you're not focused, your mind will get busy and create problems.

Why do you say I should have a goal, rather than goals?

I like to think I'm an optimistic person with an open mind, and generally I am, but I'm also realistic. I believe you can have too many goals – especially when you're dealing with anxiety and depression. If you have too many goals, you're less likely to achieve any of them than if you just have one. It's like dealing with problems. If you have a ton of problems to deal with, they're much more likely to get on top of you, so you're less likely to deal properly with any of them. If you pick out one problem at a time and break it down, you're much more likely to deal with it, and achieve exactly what you want. That's why I think having one goal is better.

When I was housebound and suffering from agoraphobia, I set a goal to walk to my local shop and buy something within seven days. Here's how I achieved it:

Monday 6th August
Step outside my door and spend five minutes in my garden.
- Achieved, so moved on to the next.

Tuesday 7th August
Sit outside in my garden for ten minutes.
- Achieved, so decided to go to my next goal the same day.

Tuesday 7th August
Walk down the road and back on my own.
- Achieved, so moved on to the next.

Wednesday 8th August

Walk to my local shop and – if I feel brave enough – walk in.
- Walked to my local shop but didn't want to walk in.

Thursday 9th August
Walk to my local shop, and walk in.
- Walked to my local shop and walked in for thirty seconds. Felt disorientated and panicky, so left.

Friday 10th August
Walk to my local shop, walk in and stay for at least a minute.
- Walked to my local shop. It was quite busy but I managed to stay for a few minutes until I had a panic attack. Walked out without buying anything.

Saturday 11th August
Walk to my local shop, walk in and buy something.
- Walked to my local shop. Walked in and picked up some milk. There was no queue, so I went to the counter and bought the milk. Walked home with a small smile on my face (and no panic!).

I had wobbly moments and feelings of panic on most of these days, but by taking it slowly and focusing on one step at a time, I was able to achieve my goal within six days. If you consider that I hadn't left my house for over three months before this, this was significant progress.

When you do something small and accomplish it, the next thing will be bigger and better. It's all about momentum, confidence and self-belief – all ingredients that will drive out high anxiety and help you achieve your goal.

Focus on what you want

As well as getting to know your 'have tos' and having a goal, it's also important to focus on what you *want*. It will help define your 'have tos', make them stronger, and set you on the right course to achieve your goal. Too many of us focus on what we *don't* want rather than what we *do* want. Remember: your focus is your future. If you focus on what you *don't* want, it's likely you'll get exactly that.

Some of the 'don't wants' (worries) that buzzed around in my head included:

'I don't want to wake up every morning with a feeling of dread.'
'I don't want to live in fear for the rest of my life.'
'I don't want high anxiety to dictate who I am.'

These are all perfectly acceptable and rational worries – the trouble was, when I focused on these 'don't wants', they became a constant fear, and didn't have any positive effect on my focus. They kept me locked in the fear cycle and fuelled my anxiety and depression.

Instead, I started to focus on what I actually wanted:

'I want to enjoy new experiences.'
'I want to feel happy, secure and free.'
'I want to be the best father I can be.'

The emotions created by my wants gave me the motivation to act. If they don't do the same for you, it's because:

1. You don't want to change, or
2. You haven't picked the real reasons why you want to change.

Anxiety and depression will challenge you, and it's your wants that will keep you going. Without strong reason or purpose, anything in life is hard. Until you understand the real reasoning behind wanting to change, there's a high probability it won't happen. You'll keep telling yourself that you don't *have* to change, and it won't form part of your 'have tos'. A person who has decided to go on a diet just to get slim will find it much more difficult than a person going on a diet for a particular reason, such as a wedding. The bride-to-be pictures herself looking fantastic in her wedding dress, while others gaze in admiration as she walks down the aisle – this gives her the motivation she needs to put down the chocolate bar. This example is filled with emotion, and it's emotion that will make you act. When you're able to touch, feel, taste and smell your goal, you're much more likely to achieve it.

If you're struggling to define your wants, it's worth spending some time thinking about them. The more they tap into your emotions, the better. Write them down and put them somewhere you can see them. They should act as a reminder of why you want to change.

Be specific

Most people's goal, if you ask them, is to be happy – and rightly so. Happiness can lead to pretty much everything you want. But how does just saying you want to be happy achieve anything? If you highlight the specific actions you could take to achieve happiness, and make these your goal, wouldn't that give you a much greater chance of success? The ultimate goal is to achieve BALANCE – but, again, that's as vague as saying you want to be happy. Be as specific as you can about achieving that goal, and ask yourself:

'What can I do today to get me closer to achieving BALANCE?'

Touch each daily goal, taste it, smell it. Bring it to life. Make it real. If it helps, put a timescale on your goal, like I did. You don't have to – this is completely up to you. If you're feeling extra-motivated, do it, but if setting a deadline makes you feel more anxious, you're defeating the object by setting it. Work hard and push yourself – just not too hard. You'll know when you're pushing yourself too hard if your goal seems unachievable.

Goals can get bigger with time and practice, but they must be achievable to help you build momentum.

Stop chasing happiness

Lots of people think that success and achievement are what bring about happiness, but what if we turned this around? What if happiness brings about success and achievement? Isn't that a much healthier way to live your life? We're all running around like headless chickens chasing success, money, fame (or whatever you believe will make you happy), when in reality these things are the main cause of our anxiety. Buying the car of your dreams might give you a quick fix of happiness, but it's only a matter of time before you go hunting for the next fix. Why? It's the way we're wired. We have an incessant need to strive for more. We can't change that (and why would we want to?), so we need to work with it.

Rather than continuously chasing happiness, why don't you start being happy, right now? The past and the future are important, but the only thing that's real is *right now*. There's no point in saying you'll be happy tomorrow – it doesn't exist yet. The book *The Power of Now* by Eckhart Tolle explains this concept in great detail. The book is spiritual and very deep, and its message is clear: you're never going to be happy unless you start to appreciate this moment and what you have right now. In other words, it's about being more grateful for what you have, rather than what you don't have. And what you have is this moment, right now.

Are you saying I should be content and shouldn't strive for more?

No, absolutely not – in fact, the complete opposite. Goals are a healthy part of life, and what give us purpose.

What I am saying is that you should regularly evaluate your goals. If your goal is to become a CEO of a large company, and you're killing yourself to get there, is it *really* worth it? Your health (mental and physical) is everything, so why jeopardise it for the sake of more money and power when it probably won't make you happy anyway? I used to work eighty-hour weeks and run myself into the ground just so I could buy the things I thought would make me happy, such as the latest sports car. Not only did they not make me happy, but the extra pressure and stress I was putting myself under just wasn't worth it. It was wrong to think I could work so many hours and still be sane at the end of it. All it did was severely increase my anxiety and depression and, in the long run, have a detrimental impact on my health.

I've met a lot of highly successful and rich people, many of whom are deeply unhappy. They have all the material goods they could want, yet many are deeply depressed and highly anxious – and spend all day wondering why they feel that way. I think I know why – they have been so busy achieving their goals that they forgot to be happy. When they finally achieved what they had set out to do, and felt that glimmer of happiness, it was too late – they were busy searching for their next 'fix'.

Stress comes as part of everything we do in life – we already know that. Good stress will push us to achieve great things. But when our body and mind are screaming at us, 'Hello, I can't take any more!', why don't we listen? We just keep going and ignore it until it becomes a condition we can no longer ignore (such as a full-blown mental breakdown). If we stop chasing happiness, and appreciate the present moment, maybe we'll give ourselves the chance to listen to our bodies and minds?

There are, of course, some people who become CEOs and who are very rich who are very happy. Some people thrive on the pressure and stress these things come with. Are these people superhuman? Maybe. Or maybe they're just being true to themselves and doing what makes them happy.

Be true to yourself

When I was young I wanted to be rich. This desire continued into my early twenties, and my only focus was on having more and more status symbols to show everyone else how great I was. To achieve this, I worked myself into the ground.

When I decided to start following my heart and simplifying my life by cutting out the bad stress as much as I could, my symptoms rapidly subsided. The constant strain in my chest would disappear for days, and only come back when I overstressed myself. I used it to gauge when I needed to take a step back. It was a sign that I wasn't being true to myself. Sometimes we have to do things we don't want to do, but the trick is to follow your heart and let it guide you. Whether you want to be a CEO or work part-time for a charity, it doesn't matter. What matters is how your goal makes you feel.

Happiness comes from being who you really are.

One of the biggest challenges we face today is being who we really want to be. We're influenced by endless external sources – the media, popular TV programmes – to wear the right clothes, drive the right car, look a certain way, and be the next A-list celeb. All of these things are driven by money, and the perception is that, the more money you have, the better life will be. I learned the hard way that this is absolute rubbish. I'm not saying there's anything wrong with wanting to have a better life (whether this is via material possessions, career aspirations or appearance). What I am saying is there's a thin line between being grateful for what you've got, and suffering from high anxiety because a celebrity has told you you're not quite thin enough. Only you know when you're tipping the balance. High anxiety and depression are normally a sign that you are.

It's OK to feel anxious about not fitting in (see the section on the DP rule), but if it's causing excessive anxiety, you need to look at why. Are you doing what you do just to try and keep up with everybody else? Are you starving yourself because a celebrity you admire is thinner than you? Is that making you happy? Probably not, if you're reading this.

Make personal pledges

Along with having a goal, I found it helped to make a few personal pledges. A personal pledge is something you believe in and live by. It's a promise you make to yourself that you never break – no matter how bad you're feeling.

I have two personal pledges I live by to this day:

1. Always be honest
It's very easy to live a lie – I did it for over ten years. I held my true thoughts and feelings back and wouldn't say what was on my mind because I was worried about how it might affect my life, and what other

people would think of me. That's why I pledged that I would always be honest, no matter how vulnerable it makes me.

2. Be open

I'm naturally a private, shy person. However, sharing my experience and talking to others was a fundamental part of my revival, and if I wanted to continue changing my life for the better, I needed to work on being more open. I got used to bottling things up. I've done it ever since I can remember, and it was a hard habit to break. My second pledge was to be more open. It's one of the hardest things I've had to do, but I've got a lot better at it. Pledging to be more open and expressing my true feelings helps me get better at it every day.

Before we move on...

By now you will have gained a better understanding of anxiety, learned some ways to reduce it, and have a clearer picture of your future. Before we move on to the final part – Ten Actions to Achieve BALANCE – I'd like to tell you why anxiety and depression revolve around two things:

1. Lifestyle
2. Mindset

The ten actions in this section focus on you dealing with these two things, because they hold the key to a balanced life. Making solid lifestyle and mindset changes will also help you overcome the fear of death and people (the DP rule) in a structured and efficient way. When you overcome these two primary fears, the sky is the limit.

The order in which you master each action isn't important. Some will take you longer than others, so you don't have to follow them in the order they are set out. Go through them individually and adopt each one at the right time for you. I don't expect you to remember and take on board each one at the same time, so keep coming back to the book if you need to and use it as a reference.

The more of these actions you master, the better your BALANCE will be.

PART 4: TEN ACTIONS TO ACHIEVE BALANCE

Action 1: Face your anxiety and depression head-on

A question I'm regularly asked – particularly by people who have suffered from anxiety and depression for a long time – is 'Where do I start?' My answer is always the same:

DEALING WITH ANXIETY AND DEPRESSION STARTS BY FACING UP TO IT.

Facing up to it isn't the same as fighting it. Although I've referred to 'fighting' on more than one occasion in this book, it means having a positive, 'get up and go' mentality rather than actually trying to fight your symptoms. You know that fighting something that is well and truly implanted in you is going to lead to bruises and broken bones, so there's no point. Facing up to means admitting there is an issue – understanding that you have a fear that needs to be brought to the surface and dealt with.

I lived in complete denial for most of the fifteen years I suffered from high anxiety. I suppressed my innermost thoughts and feelings, living a double life and not telling anybody about what I was going through. I thought I was the only person on the planet who experienced high anxiety. I felt scared, ashamed and sometimes embarrassed – what would people think? I now know this was a heavy and completely unnecessary burden to carry. Anxiety and depression are the most common of all mental health problems, with at least one in four people suffering at any one time. You are not alone.

Talk!

Revival begins with opening up, and sharing your true thoughts and feelings. Bottling up your emotions will get you nowhere. I'm not advising you to shout it from the rooftops, but please try to talk to somebody – particularly if you're holding it all inside and dealing with it alone.

The more you bottle things up, the bigger they seem.

If you've decided to talk about your true feelings, I'm extremely proud of you, because I know how difficult this can be. Opening up to friends, family and the people closest to you can be tough. This is natural because they mean a lot to you, and the last thing you want is to be treated differently by them – and you won't be. You'll be respected for being honest, and the people who love and care for you won't judge you.

It took me ten years to open up, and I sincerely hope it doesn't take you as long. If it has, get started immediately. Do whatever makes you feel comfortable. If talking to the people closest to you is a step too far, start by sharing your experience with someone neutral, such as a counsellor. Talk regularly about your true thoughts and feelings and don't bottle anything inside.

One option is to start a blog or diary. I started my blog to help me open up. I wanted to create a platform that makes it easy to share, because I appreciate it's not easy, and is sometimes the last thing you want to do. Unlike a typical forum, where there can be plenty of cynics and negativity, I also wanted to create a central point where people can find answers and ask questions, so you'll also find a list of FAQs on my site. This gives you an opportunity to get in touch, and ask a question that can be shared with the online community. Although I can't always guarantee a response, you can browse through questions and answers from others that I'm sure you'll be able to relate to. Being open is one of the biggest steps you can make towards your revival, and it would be great to hear from you.

Delegate

My first taste of delegation came when I asked my partner to help me paint my house. I couldn't afford to hire a professional, and not being a skilled painter myself, I decided to bite the bullet and ask for her help. It was hard asking for help, because up until that point I'd always done everything on my own. The control freak and perfectionist in me made me believe that I would do a better job than anybody else, so I rarely asked for help, even if it meant doing things the hard way. I'm glad I decided to push my freak aside on this occasion – not only did my partner do a great job, but it taught me a valuable lesson. When I looked at the walls she'd painted, I noticed she'd done a better job than I had! I didn't say it at the time (of course!), but all those years of struggling on my own could have been solved if I hadn't been so controlling and stubborn. It proved that all my control freak was good for was causing me more work and anxiety.

I know I'm using a relatively trivial example here, but the same can be said about anything you need help with. Don't allow being stubborn, a perfectionist or a control freak get in the way of you finding help, whether this is painting your house or overcoming anxiety. A problem shared really is a problem halved. That's true in every aspect of your life, including your revival, so stop overstretching yourself. There are plenty of people out there who would be more than happy to offer you their help, and I'd like to think you would do the same for them. I'm not saying that you should pass on a problem because you're too lazy to do it. Ultimately, no matter how much help you get, it's up to you to solve the problem. But if there's something on your mind, it's so much easier to get it out there and delegate the problem by talking about it. I struggled with this concept for many years: I used to think that if I shared a piece of personal information I would have it held against me. Looking back now, this was a really sad place to be. Other people were a massive influence on my revival. When you can learn to draw strength and positivity from others, you'll start to appreciate exactly what they can do for you (and what you can do for them). Their different point of view, or some little thing they say that sparks a thought in you, might be the thing that makes your day much better.

I'm not a great networker, and I don't have thousands of friends, but the people that do matter to me will always give me that extra push I sometimes need. I'd like to think I offer the same to them.

Find comfort in change

I've heard lots of people describe the thought of overcoming anxiety and depression as 'scary'. Surely the prospect of living with the condition for the rest of their lives should be much scarier? The fact is, some people struggle more than others with change. It's that four-letter word again – FEAR. They're afraid of the unknown and what's on the other side, including taking responsibility for their actions if things go wrong. Fear is why a person will stay in an unhealthy marriage or relationship: they're more afraid of being alone or meeting someone new than they are of the status quo, so they settle for being miserable.

Don't punish yourself by hanging on to things that make you unhappy. Life really is too short. Rather than be intimidated by what change may bring, embrace it. When I tell somebody they need to change and face up to anxiety, I completely understand that their natural reaction is fear. It's OK to feel scared by change. Most of that fear is fear of the unknown, and the uncertainty of what a balanced life might bring (especially if they've been conditioned by high anxiety for a long period of time). It's a hard habit to break but, like all bad habits, it's well worth the effort. Believe me, a balanced life is so much better than a life filled with anxiety and depression.

What will be your turning point?

The supermarket was my turning point. It was the catalyst for me wanting to find answers – and ultimately the reason you're reading this book. What will be your turning point?

Lots of people say they want change because of their children, their partner, or fear of losing their job and house. Maybe all of these things played their part in why I changed, but no matter how much they meant to me, real change was only ever going to come when *I* decided it was going to happen.

Who am I to tell you that you need to change if you don't want to?

You might have cocooned yourself in a life that has adapted itself around high anxiety. High anxiety might have made you believe that you can't live without it, creating a comfort zone that you can't step out of. You might think, 'Who am I if I'm not anxious?' If this is accurate, consider two things:

1. How comfortable is your comfort zone?
2. How happy are you, really?

If you're not free (by 'free' I mean not allowing high anxiety to dictate your life), you're not as happy as you can be.

Deciding to make a major life change is the easiest decision you can make, yet it's the hardest thing to do. I know this first-hand, which is why I'm so keen to help you do it – I know if I can help you with *your* decision, you'll never look back.

There will always be a turning point, and that will be unique to you. Mine started with me making a decision that every day was going to be better than the last. By sticking to that decision, happiness quickly crept back into my life, and I started to look forward to things in life again, rather than dread them. I know many of you will be keen to find out how long all this took. That's understandable. When I made the decision to change, and stuck to it, changes were *immediate*. And, like anything else in life, if you continue to work at achieving BALANCE, and expect the inevitable highs and lows along the way, you'll be well on your way to revival.

Action 2: Look at your lifestyle

With the benefit of hindsight, I can say the lifestyle choices I made did absolutely nothing to help my anxiety and depression. My general health and wellbeing were poor. At the time, I could blame naivety and lack of education for my choices, but that's not a good enough excuse. The truth is, I should have done more to make change happen, worked harder to stop my bad habits, and put an end to my dead-end routine.

At the peak of my high anxiety, my typical day looked a little like this:

Late morning
I wake up and instantly start having thoughts of worry, stress and dread, feeling exhausted due to lack of sleep. I stay in bed because I don't want to face the world.

Lunchtime
I've gone without breakfast so I try to eat a little bit of lunch, usually something quick and unhealthy because I don't have the energy to prepare something decent.

Afternoon
I've got no motivation to work, but the fear of losing my house and not being able to pay the bills kicks in. I can't focus because I'm stressed and exhausted. I return to bed because I don't feel great.

Evening
I distract myself from feeling anxious by watching television or playing on my Xbox. I have a glass of wine to try and relax, which leads to another glass, until the entire bottle has gone.

Early hours of the morning
I continue watching television. It's getting late so I go to bed, desperate to get some sleep. I feel tired but it's just not happening – racing thoughts of worry and stress continue to whiz around in my head. I get out of bed, put the television back on and watch it until I can't keep my eyes open any more, eventually falling asleep on the sofa from exhaustion.

Looking at this pattern, it's unsurprising that I suffered as much as I did.

I had no focus.
I ate unhealthily.
I drank too much alcohol.
I didn't exercise.
My sleep pattern was awful.

And this was just being at home. Work was just as bad, full of pressure, stress, and anxiety. Going into the office gave me the same nightmare feeling I used to get when I didn't want to go to school. A feeling of dread, particularly on Sunday evening, would consume me, and I wouldn't be able to sleep, so I'd be exhausted on Monday morning (not the best way to start your week). My phone would ring and I wouldn't want to pick it up. My inbox would fill up with unread emails. A client would request a meeting, and meeting people was the last thing I wanted to do, because I always felt 'strange' in unfamiliar social environments. I'd drink copious cups of coffee throughout the day to try and stay awake. I'd often skip lunch and, if I did eat, it would be fast food from the local van. I did absolutely nothing to help myself, and allowed this unhealthy cycle to continue. The only way I could achieve BALANCE was to significantly change my behaviour.

What does your day look like? Spend five minutes reviewing your lifestyle, from when you wake up to when you go to sleep. It might help to write it down. If there are similarities with how my lifestyle used to be, is it a surprise to you that you live in a state of high anxiety? Anybody living this type of lifestyle shouldn't expect anything less. I don't know how I can explain it better than to say:

NOTHING WILL CHANGE UNLESS YOU CHANGE YOUR BEHAVIOUR AND BAD HABITS.

I don't doubt the ability of anxiety and depression to keep you locked in this pattern, but you have to understand: you are the person you are right now because of how you live your life. Unless you're prepared to help yourself (which requires making changes and putting in effort), your life will stay the same.

Take responsibility

I used to blame external factors for my stress and anxiety. It's only when I appreciated that I created my own environment that I started to take responsibility for my life. This included being responsible for the people I chose to have around me, for my own actions, for the job I did, and for how I chose to live my life.

Partner | Husband | Wife

High anxiety can put a lot of strain on a relationship, which sometimes leads to ultimatums like, 'Either you change or I'm gone'. Is this fair? I think it depends on the circumstances. If you make no effort to change and your partner is expected to adapt to life around your high anxiety, then, yes, I think they're within their rights to want change. Living with somebody with high anxiety is challenging, especially if the condition restricts everyday normal activities, like going to the shops or taking your child to the park. A good, loving partner will always want the best for you (and themselves). It's not selfish of them to want you both to enjoy new experiences. Living a normal, active lifestyle is the only way you can do that. That's part of what makes a good relationship work. If you're not making any effort to change, why should they put up with it? Sometimes a bit of tough love is exactly what's needed.

In a supportive, loving relationship, your partner might make an effort to understand your condition further in order to offer constructive support. If this is the case, don't be upset or frustrated by their lack of true understanding. They've made an effort to understand and support you, which is the most you can ask for. Unless your partner has experienced high anxiety first-hand they will never *truly* understand, and if they've never been exposed to it, knowing what a horrible and debilitating condition it can be, would you *want* them to fully understand?

If, however, you're making a genuine effort to change, with every day getting better than the last, and your partner continues to make you feel guilty about your condition and doesn't give you a fair amount of time to make changes, you should ask yourself if you're with the right person. Are they helping you achieve BALANCE – or getting in your way?

It's natural to disagree from time to time in a healthy relationship, but if stress is caused by continually arguing with your partner (about your condition or any other issue), you're not only choosing to argue, you're also choosing to react to it with excessive stress – which won't help. An unsupportive partner will jeopardise any progress you make, and it will take you a lot longer to achieve BALANCE. All relationships are hard work, whether or not anxiety and depression are in the equation. If your relationship is worth fighting for, and if that means change, then that's what has to happen (sometimes on both sides).

Work

If you take on a heavy workload that causes you excessive stress, it was your choice to take on the workload and react to it in that way.

'If I don't take on the extra work, I might be fired.'

Even if that is true, the responsibility still comes back to you, for three reasons:

1. You're choosing to work for a company that gives you an excessive workload.

2. You haven't challenged the fact that you have an excessive workload, which might be reduced if you talk to your boss.

3. You're willing to work yourself into the ground to get the promotion or bonus you want, but you're not willing to accept the stress it brings.

The same applies to any workload you take on, heavy or light. If it's light and manageable, but still causes you excessive anxiety, then it's the type of work you do that's the issue. You have a choice whether or not to continue to work for the company you work for, and do the work you do. Getting a new job or changing your career might present new challenges and stresses, but if you believe your workplace and/or workload is the main cause of your anxiety, find something else. The stress of getting a new job can't be any worse than your current stress. The only thing you need to consider is the fact that the grass is rarely greener. If you go for something new, do as much research into it as possible first to make sure you're not jumping from the frying pan into the fire.

Is a fear of facing your boss preventing you from lessening your workload? Again, how bad can it be compared to the stress you're already under? You might think it shows weakness if you go to your boss and tell them that your workload is too much, but that's not true. Not being afraid to challenge the status quo demonstrates great strength. Plus, you probably have a genuine case to make. What if you're being exploited and you need to stand your ground? It could just as easily be a genuine mistake, and informing your boss might result in your workload being halved. What's worse, continuing to burden yourself with a stress-inducing heavy workload, or putting your fears aside and having a quick chat with your boss to see if the issue can be resolved?

'Don't be afraid of your fears. They're not there to scare you. They're there to let you know that something is worth it.'
- C. Joybell C.

Ambition and competitiveness are common traits for high anxiety sufferers. I know they were for me. I was willing to do whatever it took to be the best, get promotion fastest, and win the biggest bonus. It seems inherent to want to outperform the competition. A game of tiddlywinks can turn into all-out war! If you're working yourself into the ground, does it surprise you that you're suffering from high levels of anxiety? It shouldn't. It's no coincidence that people in jobs with a lot of responsibility (such as doctors, teachers and fire-fighters) suffer the most from mental health issues. There is, of course, nothing wrong with having ambition, but if you're not dealing with the stress that unavoidably comes with it, getting to the top will become a health hazard for you.

Like your choice of partner, your choice of job is up to you. Your career is important, but not as important as your health. Sometimes you have to put your ambitions on hold while you concentrate on you and your health. Or you can stick to running yourself into the ground. The choice is *always* yours.

Medical conditions

Suffering from ongoing medical conditions (such as asthma or diabetes) will undoubtedly make your battle with anxiety and depression harder. Symptoms can cross over, such as breathlessness and light-headedness, because they share similarities with symptoms of high anxiety, which means they can contribute to the fear cycle. However (you knew there was one coming!), medical conditions, treated correctly, should not be used as a reason for the existence of high anxiety. Lots of people live with medical conditions without suffering from high anxiety, so it's not the medical condition that is the issue.

If you suffer from any medical condition, you will have to work hard to disassociate its symptoms from those of high anxiety. If you continue to blame the medical condition for the fact you have high anxiety, it's as good as saying it will always exist – which isn't true.

Modern living

Would you prefer to sleep on the floor of a cold, dark cave, worrying about wild animals coming in to eat you, or switch your light on, put your heating on, and go to sleep in your comfortable bed in your secure home? When it comes to dinner, would you prefer to spend hours hunting for your own food, or pick up the phone and have your food delivered to you?

Since man has walked on the planet, we've had stress to deal with – just different types of stress. We can't blame modern living – including TV, the internet and mobile phones – for anxiety. If these things didn't exist, there would always be something else in life that creates stress and anxiety. There's only one thing you can really blame, one thing that all these examples come back to, and that's *you*!

AS LONG AS YOU PROVIDE AMMUNITION (IN THE FORM OF A REASON OR EXCUSE FOR IT), HIGH ANXIETY WILL CONTINUE TO EXIST.

I know I've been a little harsh in this section but, as I said previously, sometimes we need a little tough love to push us in the right direction. Every now and again we need a wake-up call – a reminder that things need to change and they're not OK as they are.

'I'm not telling you it's going to be easy – I'm telling you it's going to be worth it.'
- Art Williams

It might be hard to see at the time, but you *always* have a choice. Other options might create their own challenges and stresses, but you always have more than one option. I'm not saying you should run away from all situations that cause stress – just take responsibility for how you deal with them. Even a healthy, balanced life will always include stress, so the solution is to manage it better, not avoid it.

When stress is excessive, take responsibility and do something about it. Don't be a victim of high anxiety. If you have the mentality of a victim, you never take responsibility – it's always someone or something else at fault. When it's never your own fault, you can't do anything about it, so you'll never deal with it and be able to move on.

Anxiety didn't choose you, but by not taking responsibility and accepting it as part of your life, you're choosing anxiety.

Blaming others and making excuses will change nothing. It's only when you take 100% responsibility for everything in your life that you will see what needs to change. Until then, overcoming anxiety and depression is impossible.

Action 3: Pay attention to your environment

Why do you think free-range chickens produce better eggs than those kept in battery cages? A healthier environment means a better quality of living, a happier life, and a more balanced you.

Take pride in your appearance

Because anxiety and depression go hand in hand, the cycle of feeling low and unmotivated can lead to less interest in personal hygiene and appearance. I know it did for me. The trip from my bed to the shower sometimes felt like a climb up Everest. Although the lack of motivation and energy can make things tough, it's important to try to shower daily, even if you don't feel you need to. Even if you don't have any visitors you need to look smart for – have a shower. Even if it's a 'lazy Sunday' – have a shower. Why? Feeling clean and refreshed gives you purpose, even if you haven't got any plans for the day. The more you don't shower, the more you're reinforcing your lack of purpose and telling your subconscious it's OK not to do it (see the section on the fear cycle).

You don't have to prepare yourself for a photo shoot every day, but if you make an effort with your appearance, you'll feel much better about yourself. The psychological difference between lazing around in your pyjamas all day, compared to putting on your best outfit, is immense. Making an effort gives your self-belief and confidence the boost it needs. Even if you don't feel like you need to or want to make an effort, do it anyway. Treat yourself to that shirt you saw in your favourite shop, or those glam shoes. You're worth it.

Employment

For those of you who work, how do you feel about your job? Given a choice, I appreciate most of you wouldn't work at all, and you'd probably spend your time on a Caribbean island. Unfortunately, most of us haven't got that option! I speak to many people who describe their job as their number-one source of anxiety. I'm not surprised. If you have a full-time job, you spend most of your time at work. If you're not happy there, this makes it a significant contributing factor to levels of anxiety.

There are a very small percentage of us who actually like the work we do, and a higher percentage who dislike their boss. A bad boss can be the cause of great depression and anxiety, and unfortunately there seems to be enough of them to go around the equator, twice. If this is accurate for you, I'll give the same advice I gave previously – if you can't do anything about your job, change it. I wouldn't advise leaving a job without having another job to go to, however. Unless you're financially stable, it's counterproductive, and will cause more stress. Be sensible, and don't make any rash decisions before considering your future first (including the grass greener/frying pan to fire scenario). However, sometimes taking a leap of faith (such as changing your job) is just what you need to make a positive change. If you're lucky enough to love and enjoy your work, I congratulate you. You are in a very exclusive club, and one you should cherish. You're already ten steps ahead when it comes to achieving BALANCE.

Smoking

I smoked for over fifteen years, and one of the best decisions I ever made was to quit. I won't sugar-coat it: it was tough, but it was worth it. I did it cold turkey, but there are lots of aids for stopping smoking on the market that will help. I could go on about the many negative effects smoking has, but you already know about them, so I want to concentrate on the most important factor:

QUITTING SMOKING REDUCES ANXIETY.

Despite the general belief that smoking reduces anxiety levels, it's proven that people actually feel less anxious once they've quit. I can certainly testify to this. Anxiety doesn't need any help from other factors, and the last thing you want to do is fuel it further. Smoking does exactly that, and can increase feelings of anxiety by making you feel dizzy (being light-headed), and give you other symptoms, including heart palpitations, a tight chest and nausea. These symptoms can lead to panic attacks and further high anxiety.

There are many reasons that why quitting smoking was one of the best decisions I ever made, and preventing anxiety-related symptoms was just one of them. If you smoke, make a huge effort to quit – you won't regret it.

Alcohol

The amount of alcohol you consume should be decided by common sense, and common sense should tell you to drink in moderation. Lots of people unwind and enjoy a few drinks at the weekend, but when it's used to sedate the effects of anxiety, it's likely to lead to excessive use.

At the peak of my high anxiety, I was drinking a bottle of wine a night to help me 'relax'. I didn't need to look at government guidelines to confirm that was excessive. Alcohol was a significant factor in my fear cycle, particularly the effects of the dreaded hangover the next day. A hangover caused some of the most unpleasant physical and mental symptoms I experienced. Fatigue, headache, dizziness and vertigo were just a few of the incapacitating physical symptoms it caused.

Excessive alcohol can literally drain the life out of you, and with no energy to fight the feelings of high anxiety and depression, overwhelming thoughts of despair can take over. One person I met described a hangover as like trying to climb out of a well with no energy: 'The harder I try to climb up the well, the more I slip back down, until I'm so exhausted I stop trying. I sit at the bottom of the well, scrunched in a ball, waiting for somebody to come and rescue me.' I don't think I could describe a hangover + high anxiety more accurately.

Try to cut alcohol completely out of your life during the rebalance period. Please don't jeer at me! I'm not trying to be a party pooper; I'm giving you what I believe is sound advice based on what helped me. I enjoy a few drinks with friends, like the next person, but when alcohol was having a negative effect on me, I avoided it completely. It took great willpower and strength, but the results (BALANCE) were worth it. Just because it's legal, and your friends drink, doesn't mean you have to. Like any drug, alcohol is not the answer to dealing with high anxiety, for several reasons, including the long-term damage to your health. Establish your BALANCE, and then drink in moderation (if you want to). See – I'm not a party pooper!

Illegal drugs

Back to being a party pooper…

Coping with the effects of high anxiety and depression is sometimes like trying to stop a rabid dog from biting your arm off, so seeking relief can sometimes lead to an addiction, including to illegal drugs. Like alcohol, drugs can cause extreme feelings of paranoia, and make you feel very ill, worn out and desperate – all symptoms that fuel the highly anxious and depressed mind.

If you're taking illegal drugs to relieve your symptoms, you're doing it with a very short-sighted view. It should be obvious to you that they're not helping your levels of anxiety and depression in any way and, over the long term, they will do you some serious damage.

Lecture over. Do the right thing and get the help you need.

Special attention

If you feel that you need professional help to quit any form of drug (legal or illegal), act immediately and get the help you need. You don't have to struggle alone, and help is ready and available to anybody who wants it. A good place to start is your doctor, who will refer you to the right people.

Action 4: Control your diet

I'm not a health freak, and I'm one of the first people to say you should enjoy the finer things in life (including food and drink). But when I started to control my diet, my life changed. I've never dieted, but since I started paying attention to what I ate, and when I ate it, I noticed that my anxiety dropped dramatically. I put this down to a number of reasons, including the fact that diet plays a significant role in how you feel. Control your diet and it will change your life.

Anxiety and food

For many people, there is a strong relationship between anxiety and food. Whenever I ate, digestion was a big issue for me. I would go as far to say it was the top contributing factor to both my physical and psychological symptoms. I would panic at the thought of having a coffee or eating a meal that might give me indigestion. I used to associate indigestion with heart problems, which triggered my anxiety. Improving my diet and sorting out my digestive issues allowed me to break the psychological correlation between indigestion and heart problems, which made a huge difference to my life.

Without going into all the technical details, anxiety affects the digestive tract (the route food takes through your body) and the processing of food. When you consume food, the process of digestion starts with your brain (not your stomach or mouth), which is why so many anxiety sufferers also suffer from digestion problems. Your brain prioritises the survival instinct (fight or flight), which slows down the digestive process, often causing indigestion. The same goes for your sex drive. You have a loss of libido when you're anxious because your brain shuts that process down, putting all your energy towards keeping you alive. When you need to run from a wild animal, the last thing you need to do is eat or have sex. (Unless that wild animal is a sloth, in which case you probably have time to do both.)

Indigestion (which I'm sure you've suffered) is a very uncomfortable feeling. For me, as for many people, it manifested as a tight sensation in my chest. It was easy for me to think there was something more sinister going on. If you spend hours online searching 'chest pain', like I did, it will scare you half to death. Indigestion alone can be a significant cog in the fear cycle.

INDIGESTION = POTENTIAL HEART ATTACK = FEAR/ANXIETY

The ultimate goal is for you to feel good, internally and externally, because when you feel good it doesn't give anxiety and depression much to work with. If you want to give yourself the best chance of feeling good, inside and out, you have to control your diet to limit the chances of getting indigestion and other food-related nasties. (You know the ones I mean – they normally involve wind.)

Avoid stodgy foods

Avoid stodgy foods, or anything that is hard to digest – such as a huge curry or big Sunday dinner. Don't eat to the point you can eat no more! Carbohydrates like potato, rice and pasta are all very filling, and spicy food can make you feel very uncomfortable and cause indigestion. Maybe there's a particular food that just doesn't agree with you? Avoid it. For some strange reason, cucumber doesn't agree with me (I know – it's 96% water – wimp!), so I avoid it.

I love food, and that won't change. Don't obsess *too* much about what you should and shouldn't eat, but stodgy, carb-rich food will bring you down, make you feel uncomfortable, and aggravate your BALANCE. Food is there to provide you with energy and make you feel energised – it shouldn't do the opposite. Focus on eating consistently healthily, and if you want to lose a few pounds, do it sensibly by dropping 'treats' from your diet. Don't crash-diet – such diets never work. Start simply by searching for healthy recipes online, and have a bit of fun building a portfolio of your favourites.

I know that, when you get home, all you may want to do is sit down and relax, stick your dinner in the microwave and wait for the ping – but convenience meals don't cut it. Their ingredients, and the way they're made, stored and preserved, mean that they'll never be as good for you as eating a freshly prepared meal. Eating healthily does require extra effort, including a bit of extra prep time, but it doesn't take long to get into a routine. I found it helped me to make up a batch and freeze it. For example, when I make soup, I'll make two or three variations at the same time (in large pots) and freeze it. All I then need to do is defrost it when I want it. You can do the same with sauces, or any dish that can be frozen.

If you're struggling, there's lots of information you can find or experts (including dieticians and nutritionists) who can help you. Ask your friends for recommendations, search for them online, or find them in your local directory.

Can't look at food?

At my lowest points, I couldn't even look at food without feeling nauseous. Eating became less of a priority, and I lost over a stone in just a few weeks. That was a big problem, because we all need to eat, to give our bodies and minds the fuel we need to live. Not eating kept me trapped in the fear cycle. The more I didn't eat, the weaker I became – both mentally and physically. I knew I had to come up with a solution, fast, otherwise I would continue to dwindle away and not give myself any chance to fight. The solution I came up with was protein shakes.

When I couldn't stomach food, or even look at it, I was able to drink a protein shake and get energy from that. They're not just made for vein-popping bodybuilders – some are made for dieters. It's a big market and there's lots of choice. Decent protein shakes contain most things that a meal can offer, but they're not a substitute for vegetables and fruit, so if you can eat some foods, try to make sure you choose fresh, healthy options. I don't recommend shakes as a long-term option, and I only used them at my very lowest points, until I was able to pick up those chopsticks and re-enter the fabulous world of food.

Changes to diet

Noticeable changes to your diet will affect your BALANCE. If you're a constant fad dieter and eat meat one week and only vegetables the next, you're not giving yourself the best chance of achieving BALANCE. Your body reacts to changes in your diet, so try and keep it simple and consistent. Although it was a little boring, I stuck to set meals that included the same food every day for three months. If I wanted to make changes to my diet, I'd introduce them slowly to allow my body to adjust.

As I mentioned, I'm not a health freak, and I'm certainly not an expert when it comes to diet. However, healthy eating is about using common sense. I know that if I ate a sausage baguette every morning, followed by sandwiches, chocolate and crisps for lunch, then chips and a burger for dinner and cheesecake for dessert, all the while gulping down fizzy drinks and copious cups of coffee and having a sneaky cake at 10pm every evening, it wouldn't be long before my clothes didn't fit any longer. That's going to make me feel sad and depressed, and will probably make me comfort-eat more, and the cycle will continue.

Ultimately, you have to make a choice. Do you want the short-lived high that comes from eating a slice of cake, or a lifetime of feeling healthy and happy?

Diet tips

While on my three-month rebalancing routine, I stuck to these tips. I found that they helped me so much that I now follow them daily.

Eat breakfast
Anxiety will deplete already low levels of energy, so you want to make sure you start your day off right. Breakfast helps fuel you from the get-go, making it the most important meal of the day. Choose something high in energy like granola or porridge, and include a banana.

Cut out caffeine
If you think caffeine helps to wake you up, you're wrong. All caffeine does is bring you back to the state you should already be in. Yes, it's a stimulant, but you don't need it. All caffeine is good for is fuelling anxious thoughts. Be aware that tea, like coffee, contains high levels of caffeine. Ideally, seek alternatives like decaffeinated drinks and herbal teas.

If you can't imagine a life without caffeine (and I'm including this section because there are plenty of people who think this), the theory of BALANCE means you should be able to do what you like, including drinking caffeine. My advice is to do your best to cut out caffeine in the rebalancing period (around three months), because it's highly likely, in your anxious state of mind, that caffeine will have a negative effect on you. Like anything else, if you choose not to change your habit and continue to drink caffeine, please don't waste your time wondering why your anxiety isn't improving. Change often means sacrifice. All sacrifices are harder to make at the start, but get easier with time.

Drink lots of water
Drink lots and lots of water throughout the day. It flushes the toxins out of your body and gives you energy – which compensates for the fact you might visit the toilet a little more frequently.

Snack at regular intervals
Keep your energy levels consistent throughout the day by snacking at regular intervals. Snack on nuts, vegetables, fruit or any food that is high in energy.

Eat bananas
Potassium in bananas helps to balance the sugar levels in your blood, and the carbohydrates in bananas help keep energy levels consistent, so try to eat two or three spread across the day. I appreciate that eating lots

of bananas isn't easy, but make an effort to eat at least one (in the morning). You can also vary it a little by eating other foods that are high in potassium, such as deep-sea fish, yogurt and avocados.

Juice

I struggle to fit the recommended five portions of fruit and vegetables a day into my diet, so I came up with a solution – juicing. I have a set vegetable juice I drink every day that includes:

- a handful of kale
- a handful of spinach
- a stick of celery
- five medium carrots
- an apple.

It takes me fifteen minutes to make, and seconds to drink. My big tip is to get a decent juicer. Cheaper juicing machines tend to make a mess and don't do a great job. Try not to juice too much fruit, because it's not good for you (I'm told it has something to do with the high sugar content). If you find an all-veg juice not sweet enough, add an apple. Experiment and see what you prefer!

Cut out junk food

Eating too much unhealthy junk food will slow you down, reduce your energy levels and make you feel sluggish – the perfect breeding ground for anxiety. It's also worth noting that spicy food can increase anxiety. (Like caffeine, it can produce symptoms associated with panic.) I've never fully trusted fast food for a number of reasons, including animal welfare and what actually goes in the food, so it's easy for me to avoid it. I can appreciate its convenience, but it can be just as quick and easy to prepare healthy, nutritious meals at home.

If you do decide to treat the kids at the weekend, or avoiding fast-food outlets is impossible for you, most chains have picked up on the fact that people want a healthy alternative to their triple decker, double- bacon-and-blue-cheese special burger. For example, you can buy a salad bowl at Subway. These can be just as fulfilling as one of their foot-longs. They fill you up, they're a lot healthier, and they don't make you feel as bloated –

all perfect for reducing anxiety, increasing your energy and achieving BALANCE.

Chew your food and eat more slowly

Make your food easier to digest by chewing it more and eating more slowly. By chewing more you also trick your brain into thinking you're eating more than you actually are – which is great for losing a few pounds.

Get a good night's sleep

Your body needs sleep for effective digestion. Poor sleeping patterns (or no sleep) will disrupt the process and aid the fear cycle. The average amount of sleep an adult needs is eight hours, although we're all different, so you should gauge what you need based on how you feel when you wake up. Sleeping too much, or too little, will not only affect your digestion, but also cause other anxiety-related symptoms.
If you choose to prioritise any of these tips, it should be this one – without it, none of the other tips are useful.

Action 5: Get addicted to exercise

I'm sure you've heard it before. You've probably heard it so often that you're tired of hearing it! I appreciate that. But before you skip this action, let me tell you why exercise should be part of your routine, and why it's so crucial when it comes to overcoming anxiety and depression. It can be summed up in one word: ENERGY!

What can you do without energy? That's right – nothing. And by doing nothing, what are you accomplishing? You're definitely not putting your body and mind in a state that will enable you to deal with challenges, including the ability to overcome anxiety and depression. Low energy is a major cause of depression (see the section on the Rebalance Scale). Exercise is absolutely crucial if you want to keep your energy levels up and keep depression at bay.

There are endless benefits to exercise. Good mood is just one of them. Happiness is the key to good mental health, and exercise offers a direct route to it. Physical exercise produces chemicals in the brain that make you feel happy and relaxed, at the same time as reducing anger and stress. Self-esteem and confidence also increase with regular exercise. When we look healthy, we feel better about ourselves, and when we feel healthy, we're less anxious. Plus, the gym isn't just about exercise. It's a whole new way of life – if you want it to be. It's not just running machines and lifting weights either – there is a wide range of classes to choose from, including Zumba, various types of dance, boxing (which is ideal for releasing tension and aggression), tai chi and yoga (which are also perfect for releasing tension and shaping up). If your gym has a pool, swimming can be the ideal exercise to add to your routine. All of these things are great for your morale and for meeting new people. Some gyms also offer places to eat, crèches and play areas for children – all great for socialising. Most gyms offer free health checks and personal training sessions, so if you haven't been for a while, these will help give you a goal to aim for. Most importantly, going to the gym means you're taking time for yourself.

Exercise doesn't have to mean expensive gym memberships and equipment, however. You don't have to spend a penny if you don't want to. You can find plenty of exercise routines online that you can do at home. If you can, though, I recommend getting out of the house because going to classes and local clubs is a great way to meet new people and make friends. Or take a look at what nature can offer you. Is there anything better than going for a walk or cycle in the countryside, seeing the seasons change, feeling the sun on your face, and hearing the birds sing?

No more excuses

If we all agree that exercise is essential for good health, why aren't you doing it more often? We all have a list of excuses...

'I'm too busy.'
'I'm tired.'
'I'll do it tomorrow.'

If you enjoy exercise you have a distinct advantage, but if you're like most of the population, and make excuses not to do it, you need motivation. I'm hoping this is all the motivation you need:

EXERCISING REGULARLY WILL QUICKLY AND DRAMATICALLY REDUCE ANXIETY.

There are few things that allow you to quickly reduce your anxiety, but exercise is one of them. It really works!

If you're new to exercise, but keen to give it a go, don't be surprised if you hit the treadmill and feel like you're going to vomit within five minutes. Don't worry – exercise is not evil! Your body will adjust and you'll be running free in no time. Just keep at it and take it one step at a time.

'Patience, persistence and perspiration make an unbeatable combination for success' - Napoleon Hill

I struggled with exercise at first. Lack of time was my favoured excuse. Getting to the gym is hard for me, like it is a lot of people, but rather than allow that to be an excuse, I make time by getting up earlier and exercising as soon as I get out of bed. I find exercising then is the most effective time for achieving the best results – for me. For those of you who aren't morning people, or who have children to look after or take to school, then exercise after the school run, or in the evening, or whenever is most convenient for you.

The most important thing is not to get into the habit of being lazy. If you laze about all day on the sofa, you're going to feel tired. If you don't stay active, your body goes into 'slow mode'. The heart doesn't work as efficiently as it does when you're active, and you don't take in as much oxygen. When you have long periods of inactivity you send your body a message saying 'you don't need to work as hard', so it doesn't. This might sound like a good thing, but it's not. If you allow your heart to work more slowly and continue to lower your oxygen intake by being lazy, it will result in low morale and weaker muscles. This adds up to more anxiety. Low energy levels make you cannon fodder for high anxiety and depression. Regular exercise builds and increases muscle and boosts endurance. It delivers essential oxygen and nutrients that help your cardiovascular system to work more efficiently. By exercising and staying energised, you're giving yourself the very best chance of achieving BALANCE.

Try out different kinds of exercise and stick to what you like. Yoga, for example, can be more relaxing than running (unless you try out power yoga!), but has just as many health benefits. Running on a treadmill bores me, but I know how effective running can be for the body, so I go for high-intensity sports like squash. They get my heart pumping and the sweat flowing – just what good exercise should do. The most important thing is to choose a sport you enjoy and that works for you.

Sleep and digestion

Every high-anxiety sufferer I've met has had problems with sleep and digestion. It has something to do with the excessive production of a stress hormone called cortisol. An inactive lifestyle, a bad diet and a lack of exercise can make you produce too much of it, which leads to problems. The most effective way to regulate the secretion of cortisol is through exercise (along with a good diet and sleep). Digestion is improved because exercise allows food to move through your intestine more quickly, helping you avoid the common digestive complaints (including an upset stomach) associated with high anxiety.

Exercise also leads to better and deeper sleep. Be aware that exercising too close to bedtime can energise you, however, and may therefore have the opposite effect. If you choose to exercise in the evening, make sure it's at least a few hours before you go to bed.

The ten-minute trick

Do you know what the hardest thing about going to the gym is?

Lifting weights? No.

Running for twenty minutes? No.

Doing a whole yoga session? No.

Let me tell you: **GETTING THERE!**

I used to trick myself into going to the gym. I used what I called the *ten-minute trick*. I told myself that I was only going to stay at the gym for ten minutes. It worked brilliantly, because once I was there ten minutes flew by, so I did more. Usually, an hour went by and I wondered where the time had gone. I'd finish my routine, and once I'd got home and had a shower, I felt great. I continued this trick until exercising at the gym became a solid part of my routine, and as I continued to feel better and better each time I went, I didn't have to trick myself any more. Try it yourself, and I'll guarantee you'll stay longer than ten minutes. (Shush! Don't tell your brain!)

I also use my time at the gym to catch up with audio books. I put my headphones on and go into a world of my own. This not only provides me with extra motivation to go, but it also helps pass the time very quickly. Before I know it, an hour has gone by, I've listened to half my book, and it's time to hit the shower.

The best thing about the ten-minute trick is that you can use it for anything.

What's your intention?

Self-motivation is overrated, which is why most people who start reading a book won't get past the first chapter. It's a surprising statistic, but a true one. Seeing as you're reading this, you are one of the elite (well done – have a massive pat on the back!). You've already proved that you want change, so you're much more likely to achieve it. Seeing as you're one of the elite, I'm going to give you another tip that will take your motivation to even greater heights.

Whenever you feel that you need an extra bit of motivation, ask yourself: *What's my intention?*

I'm not a natural morning person, so I needed huge motivation to get out of bed. When my eyes felt as heavy as boulders, and my mattress and pillow felt like silk, this question always did the trick. It gave me the motivation I needed to jump out of bed because it reminded me I had a choice: I could either turn my alarm off and go back to sleep, or I could get up, exercise and completely change my life. What would snoozing for another hour do for me compared to the opportunity of reducing my anxiety and improving my life? The choice became obvious, especially when I started to feel the benefits of exercise.

Asking 'What's my intention?' is a straightforward way of solving a motivational issue, because it allows you to see the obvious choice. It gives you two options:

1. Don't do what you know is good for you and continue to live as you always have.
2. Do what you know is good for you and change your life.

Next time you struggle to get out of bed or need to motivate yourself to do something you know is good for you, ask yourself – *what's my intention?*

Get addicted

Action 5 is called 'Get addicted to exercise' for a reason. Given a little time, exercise has been proven to become addictive. You'll actually start to miss it when you don't do it. Your brain will stop giving you excuses and you'll actually long to jump on that treadmill or go to a dance class.

As I said previously, I found it hard work getting into a routine, but as time progressed and I continued to feel and enjoy the benefits, I did more. My exercise routine grew and it quickly became a fixed part of my life. Today, I'm well and truly addicted, and feel so much better for it. I really hope I've convinced you to at least give exercise a go (if you don't already), because it will change your life.

Special attention

There are many factors, including health conditions, that dictate how much exercise is best for you. You should seek further advice from your GP before embarking on an exercise programme if you have not exercised for some time.

Action 6: Stick to a routine

Self-control and motivation are overrated! Most people need a routine so we're not tempted to go back to bad habits. We also need to make our lives easier by not having temptation right in front of us. For example, if you want to lose a few pounds and stop eating cake and chocolate, don't have them in the house. If you want to stop drinking alcohol, get those bottles from last Christmas out of the house.

Our brains respond well to structure, so sticking to a routine and being disciplined is essential for BALANCE. The unknown is a breeding ground for anxious thoughts, so the more structure we can add to our lives, the better. If you know what the day is likely to bring by sticking to a routine, you're much less likely to be anxious about it. A lot of anxiety is caused by feeling overwhelmed. Being over-anxious means that you need focus more than the average person. When I don't stick to a routine, I get very little done. When I was doing very little I was more anxious – and so the cycle continued (see the section on the fear cycle).

Sticking to a routine will also make sure you're covering all the bases and doing everything you can to give yourself the best chance of revival. It's way too easy to slip back into old habits and skip the odd thing here and there. The trouble is, these little things add up, and before you know it, you've reverted to your old life and nothing has changed. If you know that you should plan for the next day at 6.30 pm every day, and it forms part of your daily routine, there is a much greater chance of you sticking to it. Planning things in advance makes them a priority. When I knew exactly what my routine was, it was a great stress-reliever. Isn't it a relief to know that everything you need is already mapped out for you – and all you need to do is follow it? You can have a busy day at work, spend the day with your children, or have a day out with friends, knowing that as long as you continue to follow a routine, BALANCE is being achieved.

I've mapped out a daily routine which I found ideal – and easy to follow – over the first three-month rebalancing period. I understand that, due to work/life commitments, you will have to make some modifications (such as when you start work), but try to stick to the core activity as much as possible – the more closely you can follow it, the better.

By following these few simple instructions you will instantly begin to feel more energetic, vibrant, motivated, positive and enthusiastic – key ingredients needed for BALANCE. Over time, the routine will become easier to follow, eventually becoming second nature. Keep it up, and you'll be rewarded with a lifetime of change.

STAY STRONG AND PUSH YOURSELF.
BELIEVE ME, IT WILL BE WORTH IT.

Special attention

If you choose to follow thoughts such as 'I'll stay in bed a bit longer' or 'It won't make any difference if I don't exercise today', nothing will change. Your life will continue as it is.

The ideal daily routine

Gaps in the routine should be filled by work or a focused activity or hobby.

6.30 am: Get out of bed

6.45 am: Exercise

7.45 am: Shower

8 am: Healthy breakfast (no caffeine)

10.30 am: Snack

12.30 pm: Healthy lunch

3 pm: Snack

6 pm: Healthy dinner

6.30 pm: Plan for the next day

7 pm: Wind down and relax until bedtime

10–11 pm: Go to bed.

Get out of bed as soon as you wake up
Start your day as you mean to go on. As soon as your alarm goes off or you wake up naturally, get out of bed. Don't lie in bed procrastinating – it allows anxious thoughts to creep in. Concentrate on the plan you made yesterday and go for it.

Exercise
I find that exercising in the morning before I eat breakfast gives me the best results. It also sets me up for the day by keeping me energised.

Shower

Shower every day. It's not only important for hygienic reasons, but it will refresh you and help wake you up, ready for your day.

Snack regularly

Keep your energy levels up throughout the day by snacking regularly on fruit (a banana is ideal) and nuts. If it helps you to stay organised, set your alarm or set an alert on your mobile phone when a snack is due.

Plan for the next day

You already know how important it is to have focus, and planning for the next day is the most effective method of getting it right. If the next day is a work day, plan what you need to do. If you're not at work, plan your activities in advance. Book something (if possible) and commit to it.

Find time to relax

In a busy schedule that includes family and work, it can be very easy to forget about your own needs, only to regret it later when you're overstressed and exhausted. Even if it's only half an hour, take time to relax every day. Put your feet up, make yourself a hot drink (no caffeine!), and shut yourself off from the world. Read a book, or do something that allows you to wind down. If it helps, close your eyes – and if you doze off, so be it!

Go to bed at a reasonable time

Aim to get eight hours of sleep every night. Some people need more, some less. Establish what you need by how you feel when you wake up, and aim to get that amount of sleep daily.

You can find a copy of this routine on my website at www.carlvernon.com.

Action 7: Lay your foundations for the future

There's no point in building a nice new house with a weak foundation – it's going to collapse. It's the same with your mind. There's no point in trying to build a future if you haven't laid a strong enough foundation for the present. When you believe that you can cope with *anything*, and have the ability to manage your thoughts, you'll start to build the foundation you need for the future you want.

I want to be clear on this point, so let me explain. You're never going to be able to control all the thoughts that enter your mind – that's impossible. What you can do, though, is *manage* those thoughts. You can decide what you want to do with them. You can dismiss them, or act on them. If you're dealing with lots of obsessive and intrusive thoughts (as a high-anxiety sufferer, it's likely you are) I appreciate that it can be overwhelming – to the point of making you question your own sanity. It's feeling out of control that makes it easy to forget you hold the power over your thoughts – **they don't control you**. Focus and time play their part here. If your thoughts are overwhelming, you have to realign your focus on something else (something that is real, not something your overactive mind has made up). If you're at work, focus on your work. If you're at home, focus on an activity that keeps you busy. Use Representation, and distract yourself. Don't sit there wondering why you're thinking those thoughts – focus on what's real. Given a little time, these thoughts will settle, a little like mud in water. The murkiness will disappear, and you'll get your clarity back.

The reality is, you *can* cope with anything. You've been designed with the strength and capability to do it. If you have any doubt, google Nick Vujicic. He was born without limbs, yet he's already done more than most people do in a lifetime. He's also one of the most positive and best motivational speakers I've ever seen. Sometimes, all it takes is a sharp reminder of the strength we possess, because it's easy to forget the power that we hold.

'Defeat is a state of mind; no one is ever defeated until defeat has been accepted as a reality.'
- Bruce Lee

I know that, when I was at my lowest ebb, you couldn't convince me that I could cope. I had to make the decision to do so on my own, and when I did, I started to face things with much more strength and determination. When I hit a rough patch I used to remind myself that there was *nothing* I couldn't cope with. It gave me the extra bit of belief and ability I needed to deal with the things life threw at me. It gave me the confidence to know, with no uncertainty, that any problem could be fixed. Sure, everyone has to face unexpected challenges in life – that's just part of life – but there's nothing that can't be solved.

Don't fear the future

'What if I get too anxious to work?'

'What if I become housebound?'

'What if my partner leaves me?'

As Judge Judy would say: 'If I were 5'9', I could have been a model.' 'What ifs' aren't worth worrying about – future, past or present.

The future is impossible to predict, so the real issue here is lack of control. I used to yearn for certainty and control, and the uncertainty attached to the future sent me into a frenzy of fearful thoughts. These thoughts were always unpleasant, and served as a reminder of how bleak my future looked (another symptom of anxiety and depression). When I learned to stop trying to control my future by concentrating on the present, fear was no longer an issue. Focusing on the next step of my routine was much more productive than worrying about whether I might be homeless in six months.

Focus on the present and stop worrying about what *might* happen. Nothing is guaranteed, and we can only do so much. As long as you know you're doing things to the best of your ability, what else can you ask yourself for? Stop beating yourself up – you're doing your best and that is good enough.

Be more happy

'Be more happy' is probably the broadest and most annoying statement in this book but, because it's also one of the most important, I'm going to give you a little exercise to prove its worth...

Imagine a set of weighing scales. I want you to place all the things that are making you unhappy, anxious and stressed in the left-hand pan. Draw a scale and write them down if it helps. Right now, you should be looking at a scale heavily tipped towards the left. That's why you're unhappy. You're walking around lopsided, carrying a heavy load of unwanted goods. Have another look at the things you put in the left-hand pan. Which ones can you realistically get rid of straightaway? There will be things in there you can't get rid of, so you need to start putting things in the right-hand pan to tip the balance – things that make you more happy. You might already know what some of these things are, have learned some in this book, or need to go and discover them. Happiness will naturally arise by getting the BALANCE right when you start placing more things in the right-hand pan – because most of the things in the left-hand pan will remain there.

'Life is not a matter of holding good cards, but of playing a poor hand well.'
- Robert Louis Stevenson

If you've ever wondered why someone has so many friends or why someone is so popular, then read on. Happy, positive people find it much easier to make friends and attract other happy and positive people (this is the law of attraction). You might suffer from anxiety and depression and still have a lot of friends, but the question still remains: how happy are you, and how happy are the people around you? If you are a happy and positive person it's highly unlikely fear will be a major part of your mindset, and therefore even more unlikely that you suffer from high anxiety and depression.

HAPPINESS & POSITIVITY
= NO DEPRESSION & NORMAL ANXIETY
= BALANCE

By being more happy and positive you enable yourself to think like a balanced person, which naturally creates and attracts more happiness and positivity to your life. I know this is glaringly obvious, but I'm just reinforcing the fact that life is much easier when you choose to accept more happiness and positivity in your life. It will keep coming to you in abundance and you'll get as much of it as you want. Right now, you've probably got the door closed on it – open it and let it in. The other choice you have (because you always have more than one) is to continue as you are.

I appreciate it's not easy – learning to be happy was tough for me. My natural inclination was to be miserable, so it was a hard habit to break. You have to practise and build it. If you wanted more muscly arms, you wouldn't expect this to happen overnight without working on it, so don't expect happiness to fall from the sky and land in your lap either. You have to work at it: the harder you work, the bigger it grows and the stronger it becomes.

Allow yourself to let go

I'm sure we all agree that life, with its ups and downs, is like being on a fairground ride. The only way to get the colour back into your white knuckles is to learn to let go of the handlebars. That means being able to let go. I'll take this one step further: STOP BEING SO UPTIGHT. Boy, was I uptight. At the height of my high anxiety I walked around like a caveman – my fists clenched and my eyebrows permanently squashed together. You might as well have called me Mr Serious. Life dictates that we need to be serious on occasion, but being tense affected everything I did, and how I did it. A picnic at the park became a regimented boot camp. And holidays – forget about it! If things weren't perfect from the start, my world came crumbling down, destroying what should have been great memories. Sound familiar? You and I both know this is no way to live. There's no joy in it. No peace of mind. If you want to achieve BALANCE you need both joy and peace.

'Life is a balance of holding on and letting go.'
- Keith Urban

The simple fact is, we're not going to control everything in life, so stop trying. Learn to let go when it's called for, which is more often than not. There is a big difference between wanting to take charge of your life, and expecting everything to go exactly as you have planned. If you expect to be able to control everything and everyone in your life, you're heading for a fall. There is only one thing you can control, and that's *you*. If you want change, start with yourself.

Life is unpredictable, but that's part of its charm. Why do thrill-seekers get a kick out of adrenaline-inducing activities like bungee jumping and skydiving, and others panic at just the thought of doing it? They look at unpredictability as a positive, not a negative. They're happy not being in complete control, and therefore process and channel the fear as excitement and happiness, not panic and dread. Life should be an adventure. Trust in yourself and your ability to deal with the unknown.

You always have a choice, which should give you the certainty you need to balance out the uncertainty. Just having the ability to say yes or no means you have two options. At my lowest points I'd remind myself of this fact, and it gave me the sense of freedom I needed to move on. I consistently remind myself that if I really don't want to do something, I don't have to do it – no matter what anybody thinks. As long as this mentality keeps pushing me forward in the direction I want to go in life, and I'm not doing something because I'm allowing fear to dictate my actions, it's a mindset I'll continue to adopt. So far it's allowed me to go from being housebound to travelling the world, and from being socially isolated to speaking in front of hundreds of people.

It might not seem obvious at the time, particularly at your lowest points, but you always have a choice. *If things don't go right, go left!* By adopting this mentality throughout your journey, you'll never have to feel trapped again.

Make more decisions

Anxiety filled my mind with doubt and uncertainty, which led to years of procrastination and avoiding making decisions. It was easier if I just let others decide my life for me. Was there an element of laziness attached to this? Probably. In my defence, I've always been quite an independent person, but who wouldn't want everything taken care of, especially if making a decision caused me anxiety? The obvious issue with this was the more I did it, the more I practised how to do it. Unfortunately, I got very good at it – even the smallest decision became a dilemma.

'I'm not going. Or should I?'
'What time should I go?'
'Should I go?'

Indecision was the bane of my life. Not being able to make a decision meant I never moved forward. I concentrated on the very short term and never made solid plans (such as booking a holiday in advance or committing to a contract) 'just in case'. I had no confidence in my ability to build a future – all because I allowed anxiety to dictate my state of mind.

Allowing anxiety and depression to dictate your path is a dangerous way to live. They will do their best to make you think it's the right way (including allowing others to make decisions for you), but this is only going to bite you at some point in your life, especially when you have no other choice but to make a decision yourself (like the decision to change your life).

Life is full of decisions, both trivial and important. The only way to get better at making decisions is to make more of them. Make a conscious effort to step forward and take responsibility, even if it means putting yourself out there and taking a risk. You won't always make the right decision – nobody does. That's OK. Just know you're in a much better place if you're making decisions, compared to avoiding them. With practice, you'll get much better at it.

Stop looking for reassurance

I was a hypochondriac and needed constant reassurance. I didn't care where I got it from, as long as I got it. My usual stomping grounds were the doctor, the internet and other people.

The doctor

When I was referred to a neurologist for my unexplainable and constant headaches, he told me about the two types of patients he saw on a daily basis.

1. The chronically ill
2. The over-anxious.

After a few questions and tests, it was clear to him I fell into the second category. It wasn't clear to *me*, though. I just wanted answers, and at that point, with anxiety completely entwined in my life, I didn't care where, what, or how I got them, as long as I got them. I would have accepted anything at that point, as long as it meant a diagnosis – so I could get the treatment I needed and move on with my life.

Seeing the specialist (and doctor, countless times) didn't help, because looking for answers that didn't exist was just another way for me to torture myself. That's why, until you achieve BALANCE you need to make a conscious effort not to visit the doctor unless there is a genuine medical reason. I completely understand that high anxiety can induce symptoms that make you feel ill, but being able to use rational thinking and hindsight, I can tell you that most of the symptoms I experienced were provoked by anxiety. Trust your instincts, and whenever you have an urge to visit the doctor, ask yourself if it's for a genuine illness or reassurance. The more you go to your doctor for reassurance, the less likely it is that you'll cope with things independently. BALANCE dictates that you won't need reassurance, so you have to stop asking for it.

The internet

Whenever a new symptom arose I'd be on the internet trying to find out if I was dying. The answer usually came back that I was, and should seek immediate medical assistance. The internet is a great thing, and is arguably the best invention in modern times. Use it for self-diagnosis, however, and it becomes dangerous, especially when you're feeling vulnerable. All the internet became good for, for me, was reinforcing the fact that the pain in my chest was a heart attack, and my headache was a brain tumour. That's sad, because the internet has so many more positive uses.

Mental health/anxiety-related forums can also be dangerous places. They can be populated by cynical individuals who spend their time feeling sorry for themselves. This sounds harsh, I know, but I question the motives of those who spend their time on forums rather than on revival. If you want to spend time on forums, use them to gain inspiration from stories of revived sufferers, or to share personal experiences that offer genuine help. Don't get sucked in with the cynics.

I know the sole aim of asking Dr Google is to get answers and reassurance, but searching for answers to health questions on the internet is counterproductive and, in most cases, will only increase your anxiety.

Others
Odds are that most of the people closest to you haven't experienced sustained periods of high anxiety and depression themselves, and therefore their advice can be misguided. Advice I received included:

'Get a grip.'
'Pull yourself together.'
'Oh, come on, you can fight this.'

There's nothing wrong with wanting reassurance from the people around you, but you have to be aware that they may not understand anxiety. You know that fighting is the last thing you want to do, because it leads to quick disillusionment, but for people who don't know that, these words sound encouraging.

Nobody should ever have to feel alone, and constructive support will aid revival. Support becomes unconstructive when you look for it excessively, particularly from individuals who don't *truly* understand. Be aware of the difference, and get the balance right. Speak to a professional if you need to.

Be less cynical

I found it hard to see positives in anything I did. I became very cynical and negative, which led to extreme paranoia. 'Why is he helping me? What's in it for him?' I used to think if I gave out a piece of information, particularly a private piece, it would be held against me. I've learned that this is no way to live, especially now I've experienced the benefits of being more open. Allowing others in has given me a connection with them I never imagined – plus, not trusting anyone is exhausting. The paranoia is crippling.

It's just as easy to be positive and optimistic as it is to be cynical. If you replace mistakes and things that don't go quite as planned with lessons, you can draw positives from anything in life. To get into the habit of doing this, I found the simplest way was to change how I referred to them. Instead of saying I had made a mistake, I would say that I'd just learned a lesson. Who isn't enthusiastic about learning?

Have faith

When I think of faith I automatically think of religion – and you may too. But the two don't have to be connected, if you don't want them to be. Having faith doesn't mean you have to be a churchgoer. It could be something as simple as having a role model – somebody who has achieved something you want to achieve. Great faith can be developed from this alone.

Faith can be used very much like gratitude in that it can help combat fear, and therefore anxiety. It can help you realise that you're never alone. If you have faith in a higher power, a power that connects us all, a power that dictates we're all brothers and sisters no matter our race, beliefs, and creed, you never have to feel alone again. With this belief, you can build the type of mental foundation that will support you for life.

Avoid avoidance

I mastered the art of avoidance and would avoid social events like the plague, just in case I had a panic attack. The thought of having to make an effort and talk to people was exhausting. By the time I'd spent three days worrying about the 'what ifs', I was too exhausted to go!

Like I said previously, how are you ever going to know you've overcome a fear if you keep avoiding it? If you want to keep friends, you have to socialise with them. If you want to eat, you'll have to go to the supermarket. If you want to live an active life, you'll certainly have to feel comfortable leaving your house. Don't be fooled by the short-term comfort you receive by using avoidance, or the wave of relief you get when you find out a social event has been cancelled.

You can only avoid things for so long before you have nothing left to avoid.

I spent years allowing high anxiety to dictate what, where and how I did something, and in the process lost years of enjoyment. Stop accommodating it – it doesn't deserve your time or effort. Avoid avoidance – start saying yes.

Action 8: End dependence

Back in the day, I would never leave my house without my mobile phone and bank card in case there was an emergency and I needed them. This might sound perfectly rational, but when a decision is based on anxiety (which it was), an unhealthy dependency develops.

'You can never cross the ocean until you have the courage to lose sight of the shore.'
- Christopher Columbus

On the one occasion I realised I'd left my mobile phone at home I quickly entered the world of 'what if'.

'What if something happens and I can't make a call?'
'What if I need to call home?'
'What if someone needs to call me because something bad has happened?'

These thoughts caused a panic attack and I raced back home.

If a balanced person had accidentally left their mobile phone at home it might annoy them, but it's highly unlikely to cause them to have a panic attack and race back home for it. Whether the dependence is on an object, place or person, if you want to achieve BALANCE, you have to change your perception of being safe.

The odds are in your favour

Whether or not you class yourself as a gambler, you are. You play with odds every day. Every time you walk out of your door, get in your car or go to work, you're playing with odds. The stake, in this case, is your safety. The fear of dying (the DP rule) is why most people with agoraphobia won't step outside their front door, and it's this fear that keeps the sufferer incapacitated.

If there is a chance of death each time we venture outside, why don't we all suffer from agoraphobia? Technically, we should all fear what's past our front door. We certainly shouldn't ever cross the road. So, why do most of us do these things without a second thought? We're simply playing the odds, and they are heavily stacked in our favour. If they weren't, we wouldn't do the risky thing. Humans are clever like that. We're geared to evaluate risk (consciously and subconsciously), and make a decision based on the facts. Some of us are better at this than others, however. For example, an agoraphobia sufferer isn't very good at evaluating risk. They're placing their chips in the wrong box. How do I know this? Simple. How many people actually suffer a tragedy when they leave their house, compared to how many return home safely each day? I know where my chips are going.

If you're agoraphobic (or if some other fear or anxiety is holding you back), look at the odds. Stop backing the wrong horse. It's rare for the outsider to come in. If you're risk-averse (like most high-anxiety sufferers), logic should tell you you're placing more risk on not opening the door and stepping out than you are staying rooted to your home. Stop losing what's at stake (in this case, your life), and appreciate there is more risk involved in *not* doing what you want to do than in doing what you want to do.

Here's a simple exercise to help you make a sound decision. Let's say you've not been able to leave your house for a while. The downside of you trying to leave your house and it not working is minimal, so on a scale of 1–10, it probably comes in at around 2 or 3. Now, on a scale of 1–10, rate the upside of trying and succeeding. It's a 10, right? Weigh up all your actions, and if the upside is bigger than the downside, go for it.

Manage unhealthy relationships

Sufferer: 'I don't want to go to the supermarket today. I don't feel well.'

Mother figure: 'That's OK, you don't have to go. You just sit there and I'll go for you.'

A mother figure will react to the vulnerability of the sufferer, and think they're doing a good deed by looking after them. In reality, they're seriously damaging the possibility of the sufferer gaining BALANCE. They don't appreciate that, by taking away responsibility and continually asking 'How are you feeling?', they're fuelling the condition. This is why it's extremely important that you, as the sufferer, recognise if you have this type of unhealthy relationship in your life so you can do something about it.

If this is you, don't be alarmed – it's very common. Being lucky enough to have somebody care for you so much is very special, but this type of relationship is simply no good for you. You'll go deeper into a child-like state until you expect everything to be done for you. Your independence will be obliterated, and when the person you're heavily dependent on becomes unavailable, separation anxiety will develop, making it very hard for you to cope. It's nothing to do with you as a person – it's the anxiety and depression: they want to be fed, and the mother figure is feeding them.

A healthy relationship should challenge you. If you're struggling to get out of bed, the best person to have around you is somebody pushing you to get out, not tucking you in. When it comes to overcoming anxiety and depression, tough love is the best type of love. It will feel harsh, almost as though the other person doesn't love you, but the fact that they want you to change is all the evidence you need to know that they have your best intentions at heart.

If you're brave enough, I recommend getting the people closest to you to read this section, especially if they have 'mother figure' tendencies. I can do all I can to help you, but if your environment isn't right, it will be for nothing.

Grow your independence

We've just covered relationships with others, but there's no more important relationship than the one you have with yourself. If you're not comfortable in your own company, how can you expect to be comfortable in anybody else's? Healthy relationships start with *you*. You're only going to develop them when you're confident enough to stand on your own two feet: confident enough to know that if it really came to it, you can do it yourself.

Similar to making decisions, independence increases when you keep practising and when you keep doing things independently. You'll never know if you can go to the supermarket on your own if you keep expecting somebody else to go with you. I'm not saying you need to jump straight into it. Practice makes perfect – and, to start with, that might mean getting support from somebody else. Ultimately, if you never get past this stage, you can never achieve BALANCE. While you're dependent on something (a person, an object or a ritual), you're not free.

Care, but not too much

High anxiety is ironic. On one hand, it made me care excessively about other people and what they thought, and on the other, it made me selfish because I was consumed by my own thoughts and feelings.

Caring is a beautiful human trait. However, be cautious about caring too much. I was a people-pleaser. My self-reflection was intense. Whenever I had a conversation, I would constantly play it back in my mind to make sure I hadn't said or done something that might have caused offence. If I thought I had (it happens even when you don't want it to), I would beat myself up. I would convince myself that that person would never want to see me again (serious overthinking going on). Unless you are deliberately unpleasant, most of us don't go out of our way to cause offence. Self-reflection is only good when we're using it to improve, otherwise it's just a tool to beat yourself up with – a tool we don't need. You're better off making space in your brain for something you do need.

If you're going to put yourself out there, you have to take the rough with the smooth. BALANCE dictates that there will be people who like you, and some who won't like you. If you're going to beat yourself up every time somebody argues with you, or you have a disagreement, you're in for a rough time. It's important to care about what others think of you, but if you let it rule your life, you'll never be yourself – you'll never have the courage to stand up for something you believe in.

Sometimes you need to be a little selfish to achieve BALANCE. The reason I say that is because if you're a people-pleaser, you'll need to work harder to concentrate on your revival because sometimes that may mean upsetting or disagreeing with somebody else.

I'm going to sound a little contradictory here, but you should also recognise when you're being too selfish. Anxiety can make you completely self-obsessed. Even if you're not feeling great yourself, make the effort to ask how somebody else is feeling, and genuinely listen to their reply. When was the last time you did that, and meant it? It's not only good for taking your mind off your own problems, but when you help other people you'll find it helps you to feel good about yourself. When you feel better – you guessed it – you'll feel less anxiety.

Action 9: Deal with medication

At the early stages of suffering from high anxiety and depression, I tended to avoid the doctor, mainly because I lived in denial. If I didn't see the doctor then there was nothing wrong with me, right? This trend quickly changed after my first visit, and I soon became a regular.

I got to know the doctor's waiting room very well. I could recite most of the magazines that sat on the table off by heart. They were usually a few decades old, so I also became an expert on ladies fashion of the 1970s. I jest, but I did visit the doctor so often that I started to feel guilty for taking up his time. The continuous need for reassurance was the culprit. I needed to be told I wasn't dying, and since the doctor was the only person who knew I was suffering, he bore the brunt of my concerns.

After the fifth (or maybe eighth) visit, I was diagnosed with GAD (generalised anxiety disorder) and depression. The doctor presented me with two options:

1. Medication
2. A sixteen-week waiting list to see a counsellor.

I was adamant that I didn't want to take drugs. I think that was down to the control freak in me. I also didn't want to become dependent. I'd rather go through the horrible symptoms of anxiety than take a pill. But there were times when I felt I didn't have a choice – when I hadn't slept for days and panic attacks convinced me I was going to die every day – when the pain was so bad I just wanted it to go. At those times a sedative (usually diazepam and sleeping pills) felt like my only option, which is why I would never judge anybody for taking medication.

I was prescribed an anti-depressant on at least three occasions. As time passed and my symptoms worsened, I decided to take the pills. It didn't go well. About twelve weeks in, I felt like a zombie. Yes, I was less anxious, but now I was at the other end of the scale: I just wanted to sleep all day and do nothing. At that point, the pills made me so laid back you could have told me that World War Three had started, and I'd have turned over and gone back to sleep.

It wasn't all doom and gloom, though, and there were a few positives. Out of character, I accepted an invitation to eat at my partner's friend's house, just as a couple. It was actually a very nice evening. We chatted and laughed, and I showed no signs of the usual social anxiety that often stopped me from talking and having a good time. My partner commented on how different I was, and I remember thinking, 'Wow, this must be what it's like to be normal.'

Weighing up the pros and cons, I decided to stop taking the pills after about sixteen weeks (about the same length of time I'd waited to see a counsellor). I got tired of the side-effects (feeling sick, dizzy and weak), and couldn't distinguish between the world that the pills had created and what was real any more. I came to the conclusion that this was something I had to face on my own. It was a scary and tough decision, but one I don't regret.

I know medication is a very personal subject, and I expect to touch a few nerves here. As I said above, I don't judge anybody for taking medication. I've taken medication, so that would be very hypocritical of me. But having come through the other side (which included dealing with incredible pain), I know that freedom is the ultimate solution to aim for – and freedom doesn't mean depending on medication. This is something you have to decide for yourself, so don't just take my word for it. Do your own research. Do what is right for you.

The placebo effect

For me, placebos are absolute proof that we don't need medication to overcome anxiety and depression. They prove just how incredibly powerful our minds are, and that we can change our physical and mental state if we believe enough in something. If you believe you'll have to take medication for the rest of your life, you're right. If you believe you have it in your power to achieve anything you want, you're also right.

The power of suggestion is there for us all to see. People like Derren Brown and David Blaine have made careers out of it. I'm talking from experience. I was incredibly suggestible. If I saw somebody in the news with an illness, I always wondered if I had it too. If somebody promised me they would eliminate my anxiety if I bought their CD box set, I would. There's a reason why so many websites offer the latest 'miracle cure' for anxiety. As a high-anxiety sufferer, you may be very suggestible.

Alternatives to medication

There are lots of alternative herbal remedies for anxiety and depression available on the market, such as St John's wort and acalite, but I'm not going to go into the pros and cons of these treatments for two reasons: (1) herbal medication didn't work for me, and (most importantly) (2) whether or not medication is prescribed or herbal, there will always be a dependency attached to it. BALANCE means freedom: freedom to do what you want when you want to do it. Taking a pill is a mental decision, and I encourage mental strength – which includes making the right decision. For me, overcoming anxiety and depression doesn't include any form of dependency, including on any form of medication.

Should I take medication?

It's not for me to say. I'm not a trained professional and don't pretend to be. What I will say, as I did earlier in the book, is you already know the answer to this question – whatever I say. If, though, you haven't taken medication, I'd like you to consider all your options. If you're at a point where you feel you can't cope, I understand how tempting it is to think you can take a pill and everything will be better. Unfortunately, it's never that straightforward. My advice is to start with a talking therapy. See a good counsellor as quickly as you can.

If taking medication for anxiety or depression is a conscious decision, and one that hasn't been taken out of your hands, you're well enough to make a sound decision. I based my decision not to take medication on the progress I had made. When I thought I needed medication, particularly on bad days, I thought about the progress I had made, which proved I was wrong. Although anxiety was hurting me, I was heading in the right direction. Seeing my progress on paper helped me conclude I didn't need any extra help. I just needed to stay on the right path and knew that, given time, everything would fall into place.

It's surprising how different things can look when they're written down in front of you, and in the section titled 'Look for clues' in Action 10, I will show you how to use a spreadsheet to track your progress. When you have enough evidence, you'll also be able to make a sound decision.

Are you currently taking medication for anxiety/depression?

If you're keen to drop the dependency attached to medication, work with your doctor to achieve this. Let them know that your goal is to be medication-free and together you can agree the best course of action, which might include reducing your dosage over a period of time.

It doesn't matter how long you've taken medication, or how strong your dose is, anybody with the right mental attitude is capable of withdrawing from (and staying off) medication. It might not happen overnight, but you do have a choice, and if it's what you really want, you can make it happen. It might be one of the hardest decisions you'll ever make, but what did Art Williams say?

'I'm not telling you it's going to be easy – I'm telling you it's going to be worth it.'

Doctors are human, just like you. They have views and opinions that you might disagree with. Communicate, and if for any reason you're not happy, keep talking to them until you find a resolution. Seek a second opinion if necessary. Do what is right for you.

Special attention

I'm not a medical professional, and these are my personal views. If you're currently taking medication for anxiety or depression, you *must* consult your doctor before taking any further action.

Action 10: Stay balanced

Overcoming anxiety and depression is a life's journey. There is no quick fix or miracle cure. On your journey you will experience good and bad days. Bad days are unavoidable. In fact, you need the bad days to help you appreciate the good ones! They might make you feel like you're going backwards, but don't be concerned – as long as you're striving for BALANCE, you're on the right track. Whatever kind of day you had today, or have tomorrow, good or bad, remember that it's completely normal.

Within the rebalancing period I experienced what I call 'anxiety aftershocks'. Just as happens after an earthquake, these are feelings of anxiety that follow the main shock. Your brain has to adjust to a new way of thinking and living, and it's a natural reaction to change. Be prepared for anxiety aftershocks. Rather than seeing them as a negative, see them as confirmation that you're on the right track. Be encouraged by the fact that every day is getting better and better.

When symptoms subside, it's natural to go on the hunt for them, particularly ones that were frequent.

'Where has my chest pain gone?'
'Where are my headaches?'
'Why aren't I worrying about that?'

This is also part of the transition your brain will go through. Given time, you'll stop searching for things to worry about, including symptoms.

Don't overstretch yourself

Dealing with anxiety and depression is exhausting work, so look out for signs of burnout. Whenever you feel that things are getting on top of you I want you to remember that you're not alone, and as part of a healthy balanced lifestyle it's normal to have to deal with anxiety and stress.

Don't burn yourself out or put excessive stress on yourself by trying to do too much at once. I was my own worst enemy at times, and there was nobody I expected more of than myself. I would put unrealistic timescales and targets in place, and if I didn't reach them I would suffer for days (it's the perfectionist in me). When I realised it was *me* putting all the pressure on *myself*, it was surprising how quickly I could change the pattern of self-destruction. Don't fall into the same trap. As long as you're consistently taking action you're moving in the right direction, however long it takes.

Keep taking action

Starting something is the hardest thing to do, but once you get going you'll build momentum (the snowball effect), and momentum is what you need to make consistent change. The snowball will only gather speed if you keep taking action.

There is a huge difference between *talk* and *action*. I urge you to be a doer, not a talker, because this is the fundamental difference between you overcoming anxiety and depression, or continuing to live as you are. Getting to this point would be for nothing if you don't decide to act. Knowledge is power, and possessing it gives you a distinct advantage, but it's action that will effect change.

Procrastination, as you know, was an issue for me. I would sit pondering for days. In my head things were changing (talk), but in reality I wasn't doing anything to make the changes happen (action). I ended this cycle of procrastination and constant feelings of bitterness by deciding never to leave a situation without taking action. If I walked away feeling unsatisfied, it usually meant I hadn't done enough to make a change.

If you don't like what your doctor has told you – take action.

If you're tired of being housebound – take action.

If panic attacks keep beating you up – take action.

If you want to feel more alive and energetic – take action.

If you want to be able to spend quality time with your friends and family – take action.

If you want change – take action.

NEVER STOP TAKING ACTION.

The achievers in life never stop taking action, because they know action is the only way to achieve lifetime results. If you hit a bad patch, something doesn't quite go your way, or you feel like you're getting nowhere, don't stop taking action. Things will always be sent to challenge us. Ride them out – they are temporary.

Look for clues

Track your progress, so you know if you need to make a few tweaks to get things right. Like keeping a diary, keep a daily track of what, where and how you're doing things. I found the easiest way to access the information was to use a spreadsheet. I had one on my laptop so I could easily review and access the results. (I've created a template you can download from my website at www.carlvernon.com.)

For one month, rate each day from 1–10 (where 1 is absolutely abysmal, and 10 is the best day you've ever had). You should have a section for the date, day, rating and notes. In the notes, highlight anything that happened on that day (like a small diary entry). After a few weeks, take a look at your results.

Were there particular days that scored well, or badly? What were you doing?

Did you feel better on Wednesdays because you'd been to the gym?

Did you feel bad on Sundays because you had nothing to do?

Ask yourself questions based on your results and look for clues.

By writing down the reasons behind your moods, you can make the changes needed. For example, if on Monday you felt particularly anxious, write down what you were doing (or not doing) on that day. Do the same if you were feeling particularly good on Thursday. When you track what you're doing, the facts speak for themselves. Those bad days that make you think you've gone backwards are easily contradicted by actual results. You might be pleasantly surprised by your progress.

Let's say your sheet starts off with a bunch of 2s and 3s (which is very normal). Within a couple of weeks you start creeping up to 4s and 5s. You pay attention to the things that are working (and not working) and a week or so later you select 6s and 7s, until you hit the dizzy height of 8+. Those inevitable bad days are just that – rare occurrences that form a small part of the bigger picture.

It doesn't matter what your sheet looks like. The only thing that counts is that you see progress. If you don't, keep looking for those clues. If you can't find them, look harder – they're definitely there. They hold the key to your change. If you need to, go back to the ten actions to achieve BALANCE, and keep taking action. Positive change will come.

Stop and change old habits

Anxiety, being the best salesperson in the world, will continue to try and convince you to go back to old, 'comfortable' habits. Remember, these old habits give you a false sense of security. Sometimes, even if things are harder for us (including suffering from high anxiety and depression), we continue doing them because we believe that the short-term comfort we get from familiarity makes them right. (For example, the relief you get when you decline the invitation to your friend's wedding because you don't want to feel anxious in a social environment.) As I said previously, if you keep avoiding things, very soon there won't be anything left to avoid. Start thinking longer-term, and stop allowing short-term comfort and old habits to get in the way of your ultimate goal: BALANCE.

Stick to taking action, keep making changes, start saying yes, and make these your new habits.

Common sense is the greatest tool you will carry with you on your journey: use it to bash anxiety around the head. These old habits are no good for you. Continually rationalise, and don't allow anxiety to cloud your judgement. Change isn't easy, but the uncomfortable and scary feelings are only temporary. Once you break through them, with time and practice, fear and limitations will have a whole new meaning.

Here I want to remind you of my favourite quote from Albert Einstein that I used at the start of the book:

'Insanity: doing the same thing over and over again and expecting different results.'

Will your life follow the same pattern, or will you recognise that what you've been doing so far isn't working?

Change is exactly what you need. Embrace it – and enjoy it.

Are you ready?

This is such an important point that I'm going to include it in my final summary:

IF YOU DON'T TAKE ACTION, NOTHING WILL CHANGE.

So what's your plan? What action are you going to take right now that is going to start your journey of revival, and begin your change?

Here are a few suggestions:

- If you've bottled things up inside, and nobody knows about your condition, start talking and sharing. Pick up the phone and make an appointment to see a counsellor. Go to my website, www.carlvernon.com, and share your experience with me.

- Change your lifestyle by taking responsibility for your life and the actions you decide to take (or not take).

- Make sure the environment you're in is helping you work towards achieving BALANCE. If it isn't, change it.

- Pay attention to the food you're eating, and make any necessary changes to your diet.

- Make an appointment to visit some local gyms. Pick one, and start exercising.

- Think about a routine that works for you, and stick to it.

- Start building the foundation for your future by doing things that reinforce the fact that you can deal with anything life throws at you.

- Stop depending on others to live your life for you. Find the strength within yourself to make your own decisions and become more independent.

- Make an appointment to see your doctor, and talk to her about your medication, if you're taking any.

- Never stop taking action. If you feel old habits creeping back into your life, stop and change them.

Don't finish a day without taking one of these actions.

Perhaps anxiety and depression have gripped your life so tightly that you haven't taken action in a while. Doing just one of these things might be the status-quo buster that is the catalyst for more, and bigger, change. When you feel the same change and improvement that I did, I have no doubt you'll want to do more. Before you know it, you'll be the most balanced person you know and, with time and practice, high anxiety and depression will become a distant memory. They will never affect you in the same way again.

BALANCE is waiting for you whenever you're ready. You already know what it's like, and now you have the tools to achieve it again, what are you waiting for? Go and get it!

It's surprising just how fast your life can change.

Always remember:

OVERCOMING ANXIETY AND DEPRESSION IS A LIFETIME'S JOURNEY.

AIM FOR BALANCE.

NEVER GIVE UP.

Further help

If you don't want your journey to end just yet, you can stay in touch with me via my website:

www.carlvernon.com

There you'll find my blog, news about events and workshops, free resources, and other information that will keep you balanced.

I hope to see you soon!

Take care and best wishes,

Carl Vernon